Living *with* Border Collies

Barbara Sykes

✵ THE CROWOOD PRESS

First published in 2021 by
The Crowood Press Ltd
Ramsbury, Marlborough
Wiltshire SN8 2HR

enquiries@crowood.com
www.crowood.com

This impression 2024

British Library Cataloguing-in-Publication Data
A catalogue record for this book is available from the British Library.

ISBN 978 1 78500 981 5

Cover design: Sergey Tsvetkov

Dedication
To all the great dogs and handlers of the past: without them we would not have this amazing breed. Their expertise and knowledge passed down from generation to generation is something to value, and I hope I can help to keep their knowledge alive within the pages of this book.

Acknowledgements
I would like to thank Sarah Ainge for reading each chapter to make sure I didn't miss anything from my notes, my very patient granddaughter Hannah Matthews for proof reading and making sure my sentences didn't turn into paragraphs, and our brilliant vet Peter O'Hagan BVMS Cert AVP (GSAS) MRCVS for his valuable input for the health and welfare of the Border Collie.

Photos: The author, Andy and Sarah Ainge, and Ian Hughes.
Diagrams: Bev Ibbotson.

Typeset by Derek Doyle & Associates, Shaw Heath

Printed and bound in India by Parksons Graphics Pvt. Ltd.

Living *with*
Border Collies

Contents

Preface

We always want to find out more about someone or something we love, and the more we find out, the better we understand the person or object of our love. This book is about the Border Collie as a breed: to know it is to love it, but to understand it you need to know what it thinks, and why. For the ease of writing I will be referring to them mainly as 'he' or 'him' for no other reason than it can take away the value of a sentence sometimes by using 'he, she or it'. I also refer mainly to them as a collie, which was their original title and is an easier reference than using Border Collie each time. I also use the word 'guardian' rather than 'owner', for reasons that I hope will become obvious as you read the book.

My previous book *Training Border Collies* was, as the title suggests, about training, and some of the chapters can be read in any order. This book is different as each chapter contains information about the breed, and to miss a chapter could mean not fully understanding information further into the book. I sincerely hope that I have made each chapter interesting and informative enough that no one will want to miss a chapter. Border Collies are all very different, and throughout the book are photographs of different colour genes. I hope you find it interesting learning about each one. As with everything there are always exceptions to a rule, but it is amazing how accurate you can be when you study and get to know the different colours and characters.

I do refer to farmers and shepherds and the working dog, but that is where the foundation of the breed lies. They are working dogs, and if you can find the key that turns the lock into that working mind you will get even closer to understanding your own dog. I know there are some people who shouldn't have a dog both in farming and companion homes, but my experiences and writings are about those who revere their dogs.

Finally, although this book is not specifically about training, it is about understanding problems, what may have caused them, and how to solve them. Although other breeds won't have the complication of different colour genes and characters, a lot of the information in Part Two of the book will be helpful to guardians of other breeds.

PART ONE

The Border Collie:
Past to Present

CHAPTER 1

History of the Breed

Every working breed of dog has its own history. The more we know about each breed and its background, the easier it is for us to understand how to use their instincts to our advantage. An empathy with the origin of a breed can help in enhancing a partnership, and it can help with training and problem solving. While each breed may have a trait that will require a little extra patience and understanding, without those traits it wouldn't be the same dog. For example, a breed of dog that was originally bred to track and kill vermin should not surprise us when it wants to dig or go down holes. A Border Collie may want to stalk other dogs, or stare for long periods of time at your next door neighbour's cat, but these are instincts that are part of its heritage. If we try to breed them out we risk losing the very essence of what made us fall in the love with the breed in the first place. But if you understand those instincts you can redirect them in a way that is beneficial for you and your way of life, just as the shepherds did years ago.

The history of the Border Collie is a fascinating account of a breed of dog whose herding skills are just as valued today as they were over a century ago. They all have different skills and individual characters, and the mystery of these will unravel throughout the following chapters. The fact that they can vary in colour, size and general appearance can make it easier to identify and understand some of their characteristics. We need to look to their ancestors for the answers, and not just to parents or even grandparents, but often to much older relatives.

Have you ever been told that you are just like your grandmother or your aunt or uncle? Perhaps in looks or in temperament? I know I'm supposed to be like my paternal grandmother but then… what was she really like? I know one of my ancestors loved being on the water, whereas I am definitely one to keep my feet firmly on Mother Earth; however, I do love horses, dogs and farming, as did another of my ancestors. I am a mixture of both sides of my family, and am fortunate that I can trace them back, but tracing back your dog's personality can be so much easier.

A Border Collie is different to many other breeds – in fact it is the only breed that is as diverse as we are. Different colour genes carry down through generations, each one denoting different characters, strengths and vulnerabilities. Understanding a Border Collie simply as a dog is not always enough to give us that bit extra we need to really understand our own dog. They need understanding for their instincts and amazing intelligence. This is their heritage passed down through generations, and those generations probably go further back than we can imagine.

The Birth of a Breed

The shepherd's dog was first given the title of 'collie' in Scotland, but how this title originated is uncertain. It is thought it could be derived from the Scottish breed of black sheep called colley, which is quite probable, as 'colley' is an old Anglo-Saxon word meaning 'black'. However, 'collie' is also thought to mean 'useful' in the Celtic language, making the term 'collie dog' a 'useful dog'. History has played a huge part in the breed we have today, even down to the original title of Collie.

Records and archives put dogs working sheep and cattle in Scotland centuries before they became known in

Auld Hemp.

England. Archives show us that the working sheepdog known today as the Border Collie was working in Wales in the mid-nineteenth century, with the first ever recorded sheepdog trial being in Bala in 1873.

With the help of archives and recorded dates, we know that dogs have been working sheep and helping shepherds for centuries, and not all the same breed. There is recorded evidence of Beardies, rough collies and Old English Sheepdogs, so how did it evolve from the shep-herd's dog to the Border Collie we have today – a dog that is able to run sure footed and with speed over rough mountainous land, to be gentle with lambs yet able to stand up to awkward ewes, and to work in all weathers without tiring. A breed that the shepherds, who spent long days on the mountains, were, and still are, proud to call their working companion.

Have you ever stopped to wonder who decided how much of what ingredients to put into a bowl to make the

Laddie was born over a hundred years after Auld Hemp, but look at them closely and you will see there is very little difference between them.

perfect cake? If you have, you will know that it didn't just happen, and it wasn't luck: it was trial and error until the perfect cake was produced. But if the baker didn't keep a note of what exactly went into that mix, then he or she would've had to start again.

It may seem strange to compare a Border Collie to a cake mix, but the theory is the same: the mix has to be right, and you need to keep a record so you know what to add and what to leave out. Thanks to those shepherds who really understood the power and intelligence of the dogs they were working with, they bred very carefully and kept a record of the successful pairings. Those records are still being kept today by the International Sheepdog Society (ISDS), and if every Border Collie today had a known family tree it could be traced back to those foundation dogs, and to one in particular: Auld Hemp.

Auld Hemp was bred by Northumberland shepherd Adam Telfer. He was born in 1893, and his destiny, apart from being an amazing sheepdog, was to become known as the 'Father of the Breed'. There is no doubt that Adam

Telfer understood the breed, and that he knew what was needed to improve the skills of the working dog as it was then, and how to create balance when breeding for the future. In other words, he didn't just throw ingredients into a bowl to make any old cake, he looked at all the possibilities and only included what was needed, and then balanced it to produce what many have called a canine genius.

Auld Hemp was described as being of medium build, tri-coloured, and with a quiet power when working sheep. Today we can take videos of dogs working and can hand them down from generation to generation, but we have no digital record of Hemp. However, if we see a dog running up a fellside, gathering a flock of sheep and bringing them all safely home, we are looking at his legacy, and for that, we don't need to have seen him working, as his intelligence and his skill live on in every true-bred Border Collie today. While it may seem impossible that all collies are descendants of this one dog, it is a fact that all dogs registered with the ISDS can be traced back in the stud books, and at some point you are likely to find Auld Hemp at the foundation of your line.

The breed as we know it today is traceable back to Hemp, but of course he is the result not just of his parents, but also of their ancestors – of whom we have little or no records of lineage. Dogs were working sheep in England and in Wales before Auld Hemp was born, and they must have been dogs with some calibre for there to have been sheepdog trials. The trials may not have been as keen in competition as they are today, but no shepherd, then or now, will put his dog against another unless he knows it has the ability to match any competition. Any search into the past will have a point where the records can't take you any further without there being a degree of uncertainty. Historical archives prove with certainty that dogs have been working with shepherds for centuries, and a dog that was more of a herding dog than a droving dog was slowly evolving. But from that date in 1893 when Hemp was born we have records that track the breed to the present time with certainty.

Auld Hemp was soon recognized by local shepherds for his skills. I think there can be little doubt that, when travel was by horse and cart and information was bound by distance, word of mouth would have helped spread the news of this amazing dog. Knowledge of his strong but gentle working skills certainly attracted the attention of shepherds from a little wider than the usual local areas, all hoping to introduce his calm strength into their own line. As a result he is believed to have sired over 200 puppies. Now let's think about that breeding foundation for a moment: 200 puppies, sired by Auld Hemp who went on to work, and a percentage of them to breed more puppies, and all relating back to Hemp.

The foundation for the breed was there all those years ago, with branches spreading out on Hemp's tree of life. We will discover in a later chapter how important it was that the bitches brought to him were not all the same – they will have had different strengths, characters and work abilities. The Border Collie you see in a local park may appear to be just the same as the one living next door to you, but because their genes are from different ancestors, this could mean that their characters are totally different. But as their heritage can take them back to Auld Hemp, so will they have an ancestral line going back to their maternal ancestors – the females who produced puppies by him. Border Collies may vary in appearance, colour and height, but they should all have the physique that enables them to do the work they were bred to do.

If not, they will struggle to keep up with sheep, and will not have the stamina needed to be able to work on steep undulating ground for great lengths of time.

Throughout the history of the breed there have always been key dogs such as Auld Hemp who have left their mark, whether this is their outstanding working ability or their prowess on the trials field. A good shepherd who understands breed lines will know when to breed out to fresh bloodlines, and when to breed back in again: a knowledge of the ancestors of each dog means they can balance the line without inbreeding. Referring back to my opening paragraph, where I know I bear a resemblance in appearance to some of my ancestors but my character to others, some of the Border Collies of today will bear a resemblance to certain key dogs in their bloodlines. I have heard it said that few collies today look like Auld Hemp, but if we look at the two photographs, Laddie, who was born a century after Hemp, certainly looked similar to him, and also had the same quiet way of working sheep.

The International Sheep Dog Society (ISDS)

Auld Hemp, his progeny, the breed title, the archives and the records, are all part of a process that has kept that great dog's legacy going for over a century, and hopefully will continue to do so far into the future. I can understand how easy it could be to think that the Border Collie of today has no relevance to those Collies of a century ago. However, I wonder how many people say or hear the words 'Border Collie' but don't really know where that title came from. Let's take this away from dogs for a moment and refer to Florence Nightingale. I think everyone must surely have heard of her and must know she was a nurse, but without delving into her history too much, how many know why she was called the 'Lady with the Lamp'? Similarly we need to look at history to find why the title 'sheepdog', which is very descriptive, earned the title of Border Collie.

The ISDS was formed at Haddington in Scotland in 1906. For several years the Society's annual sheepdog trials were held in Scotland, with a record of just two being held in the north of England. During those early days there would still be other types of collie or working dog, and they too would probably have been competing at the sheepdog trials. In 1915, the ISDS secretary James Reid, for the purpose of keeping accurate records, chose a title to distinguish the working sheepdog from other breeds. What better title for a breed of collie that was born on the borders of England and Scotland than the one we know today, the Border Collie? Although at the time it may have been just a prefix to the word 'collie' to distinguish it from other collies, I don't think anyone could have predicted that over a hundred years later it would be a breed as famous in lands far further afield than the borders where it began.

Records of breeding have always been kept, but originally these would have been on paper and handed down to the next generation of shepherds or breeders. When the ISDS created their stud book they ensured that not only did they have all the relevant information in one place, but they were also safeguarding that information for the future. The first annual stud book was issued in 1949, but two earlier books have dates of puppies stretching back to the 1890s.

All litters of puppies with registered parents can be registered with the ISDS and their details printed in the annual stud book. I think it's important to point out that although the breed now has an official title, the ISDS still holds dear their original title. Every registration card includes both 'working sheepdog' and 'Border Collie' in the certification. We will find out later why that certification holds a huge relevance, because a dog resembling a Border Collie may not always have the ability to work sheep, but a dog that can work sheep will always be a Border Collie.

Shepherding Past and Present

There have been huge changes in farming and shepherding over the centuries, but even with modernization and machinery, one thing that has remained constant is the sheepdog. The stamina, intelligence and shepherding skills that were so important in the past are just as important now. Even in this era of technology the working sheepdog still proves itself to be indispensable.

The majority of shepherds in the past will have been hill shepherds, working and living on terrain that called for hardy sheep, strong men and determined collies. The hours of work would have been from first to last light, and in harsh winter weather or at lambing time, those hours would continue through the night. It isn't difficult to understand why the dogs that were with these men

from dawn to dusk earned themselves the title of the shepherd's working companion.

Armed with food and drink in his backpack, the shepherd and his dog could be walking the steep and often rough land for the full day. The food would have been basic and just enough to satisfy, as other essentials would also have had to be carried. Little could be done for a sheep that was hurt or in pain, or a lamb needing milk, if the shepherd did not carry the essentials in his bag.

Winter on high land is always harsher than on the lowlands. There are some amazing records of dogs finding sheep that were buried under snow, trapped between rocks, or lame and unable to keep up with the rest of the flock.

I find it fascinating that although so much has changed in farming from past to present, the actual day-to-day work for a shepherd has not. So if the sheep, the work, the shepherd and his dogs haven't changed, what has? The change is in the way the work is done and the speed with which it is completed, a progress that is enabled by the use of machinery.

I think there are many professions that we can look at and say 'that must have been hard in the past', but at the time a faster or easier way was not known. Shepherds of the past began their day carrying a crook and a backpack as they set off to check on their sheep. They could never have imagined that before they had even left the homestead, future generations would be halfway up the hill on their quad bikes. For the shepherd of the past it could have been a lonely life, but today's shepherd can be back home for lunch, and he can carry any essentials on his bike rather than on his back. Yet for all the technology and machinery, the work for our shepherds today can be just as testing.

Sheep still have to be shorn, and whether this is with hand shears or by machine, it can be a back-breaking job. Dipping, spraying or injecting to keep flies at bay, plus worming and trimming feet, are all part of a shepherd's job, past or present. In the past most of it would have been very manual, and although shepherds would have needed to be strong men, I can imagine they might have suffered with back pain in their twilight years. Today, shearing machines enable shearers to do the same number of sheep in one day that in the past would probably have taken several days. The small, stone-walled pens in the fields have been replaced by portable pens, and modern sheep farms have dedicated yards, pens and holding areas.

More advanced technology and machinery mean that farming is now conducted at a much faster pace, but the sheepdog is the one thing that hasn't changed, and which every shepherd needs.

The Sheepdog at Work

Whether on a farm as a shepherd's dog or in a companion home, the fundamental nature of the Border Collie remains the same. Understanding his development and his prowess as a working dog can provide clues to some of the behavioural traits displayed in a companion home. Although you might not be a shepherd, live on a farm, or have sheep, finding out more about your dog's background will not only help with problem solving, but also provide a fascinating journey into the mind of this amazing breed of dog.

Gathering a flock of hill sheep requires the same skills, intelligence and stamina that it did a century ago. Today's sheepdogs can now hitch a ride on the quad bike rather than walking the first mile or so, but from then on the work is done 'on the paw'. A large gather to bring several hundred or more sheep down from the hills, and often

not all from the same flock, will have several shepherds and their dogs involved. Imagine those dogs with similar commands but different whistles all working together in unity.

Without realizing how good they are at problem solving, it's easy to underestimate their intelligence, and the ability to be able work out certain situations. Sometimes we may read too much into their actions, but I believe that we should always give them the benefit of the doubt.

When a dog is a distance from the shepherd and behind a flock of sheep, he is out of the shepherd's sight. Being able to trust the dog that he will do the job he has been sent to do is a huge part of the partnership needed between shepherd and dog. Gathering the sheep together into a flock and bringing them to the shepherd is part of the instinct to herd, but driving them away again is almost contrary to those instincts. We will discover later that some dogs will be better at driving away than gath-

Meg Problem Solving

Shepherding on a large estate, I sent Meg to gather a flock of sheep. The sheep came down the hill to me, minus my dog. My husband thought she'd run too far and gone on to the road and been run over, but I had far too much trust in my dog to think that. When I arrived over the brow of the hill, there she was sitting with a sheep that was trapped in some old wire. Did she know I would come looking for her? Did she need to make sure every sheep was accounted for? Or did she sit down not knowing what to do for the best? I knew Meg, and I'm sure she knew I would come looking for her and would help her to get the job done.

Meg's ancestry goes back to the great foundation dogs; not only was she a great trials dog, but she was able to work out difficult situations in her everyday work as a sheepdog.

ering, and with different strengths, these dogs need a different approach to managing them in the companion home.

Taking sheep that were to be sold to a market in the days before cars and wagons must have been a huge task. Large flocks of sheep would be moved many miles on foot, often taking days to get to their destination. They would follow well worn 'drovers' roads', some of which are still in existence today, albeit it in name only, and there would be hostelries along the way for overnight stays. Droving was often an occupation in itself, and there are some amazing accounts of drovers paying to return home by carriage or boat but leaving their dogs to return on foot. The dogs apparently retraced their journey. They would stop at the same overnight hostelries, where they would be fed and watered before starting out again. This is not something we would do today, but at the time it was not unusual – and for the dogs, although not an everyday occurrence, it was part of their lives. I think it would also have almost been like having 'time out' for them. Making sure a large flock of sheep was controlled, didn't stray off the track, and being on the move for most of the day, would have been mentally and physically tiring. The trot back home at their own pace would probably have been a nice break for them, and who knows, maybe they took their time.

We may wonder sometimes what it would be like to be able to travel back in time, just as an observer. But I wonder what the shepherds and drovers would think if they could observe how their work is done today. Travel today is done in wagons and trailers, and destinations are reached in a fraction of the time taken by the drovers. But just as dogs were used to gather the sheep and 'drive' them from one place to another with the drovers, they now gather them into pens and help to push them up the vehicle ramps.

One thing I am sure that will be different today is the training of collies for sheep work. It takes a lot of time

A very old photograph of a group of dogs waiting for their turn to run in a sheepdog trial.

Taken at least eighty years after the previous photograph, another group of dogs waiting to compete. It is a credit to breeders of the past how little the collie has changed.

and patience, but I wonder how much, or how little, time would have been needed all those years ago. Farming and shepherding is a way of life, and in the past, the dogs would have spent all of every day with the shepherds, and although the dogs could probably gather a flock, it may not have been as necessary. The shepherd would be on the hill with them, and often working from the back of the flock, with his dog or dogs pushing, rather than herding them. It is still a way of life for shepherds today, but collies have been bred very carefully, so they can multitask. They can run out a long way to gather a flock of sheep, whether on lowland or the hills, and when the time comes for the sheep to return to their pastures, the collies are capable of driving them there, and not necessarily with the shepherd walking with them.

Like the collies, many farmers today also multitask, and as well as running a farm, they shepherd their own sheep. Modern equipment means that shepherding tasks are now more efficient and can be incorporated with all other aspects of farming. On larger farms shepherds may be employed to work with the sheep and also to work on the farm, but there are still some large units where a shepherd will be employed full time to look after a large flock of sheep. But the farmer, the part-time shepherd and the full-time shepherd all have one thing in common: the need for a good working dog.

The Ability to Focus

One of the Border Collie's many skills is the ability to focus. Once they know what is wanted of them, they are dedicated to completing the task. I often think how we, as humans, have various thoughts in our minds at once, and sometimes go into automatic pilot working on one task while thinking of another. Once trained and with

A sheep has turned to challenge Jim, but he is so focused that it doesn't occur to him that he won't succeed in turning it back.

the knowledge of what is needed, the collie will see only one thing in front of him: the task he has been set. They rarely have what I often refer to as the 'what if' outlook. If we put a collie in a gateway and ask him to stop a flock of 200 sheep from getting through the gate, it will not occur to him that he might fail. Obviously the dog needs to be both well trained and able to do the job – only a foolish person would ask someone to do a task they were not mentally or physically able to do. But once in that gateway, the dog will do his utmost to complete his task. We may be more advanced in many ways, but we often tend to safeguard ourselves with the 'what if I fail', and if we speak it out loud our manner will be one of uncertainty. The amazing thing about the confidence of a well trained collie is the fact that just standing there with an air of confidence can make the sheep falter.

With Focus Comes Power

When a neighbour's cattle got on to our land, old Rob didn't attempt to stop them as they ran across the field in a group: instead he waited until they were in a line near the fence, then he stood facing the leader. Imagine the scene of a massive four-legged cow being challenged by a dog that didn't even reach knee high. Rob held his ground, and the cattle turned round and went back to where they had come from. In a group they may have been bolder, but Rob waited until they were in single file, so his challenge was against the one in front and not the herd. Rob was so focused it didn't occur to him that they might not stop, even though he was outsized and outnumbered.

Old Rob could work sheep, and could also stop and turn round running cattle; he was also one of the kindest, gentlest dogs you could ever wish to meet.

A Bond of Trust

I was told many years ago, 'know your dog and trust your dog, and if you can't do that... what's the point of having a dog?' This is an excellent point with regard to both a companion dog and a working dog. The degree of trust required when a dog is working sheep is exception-al, because however well the handler and the dog work together, the sheep rarely have the same degree of unity. Training a sheepdog to be very obedient is the last thing a shepherd wants: he needs his dog to be biddable and to be able to work out a problem and act on it without fear of reprisal, but he also needs his dog trained to such a degree that it will do what he asks without question.

There has to be a bond of trust between shepherd and dog. With a large of flock of sheep separating them, each must have complete confidence and trust in the other.

That sounds contradictory, and in a way it is, but once explained you will see just how intelligent collies are and understand the amount of trust needed for a good partnership.

A shepherd can send his dog out to gather a large flock of sheep and he may give his dog a whistle to go to the right, but the dog doesn't take that command, instead he goes to the left. The dog is at the back of the sheep and can see what is happening, but the shepherd cannot see what the dog can see. The shepherd thought there was a problem at one side of the flock, but the dog knew that a sheep on the left side was about to break loose. The dog goes to the left, brings the errant sheep into check, and then goes back to see if he's needed on the right. That same dog can go on a sheepdog trials course and take every single command the handler gives him.

I have trained a lot of dogs to work sheep, but I cannot explain exactly how this relationship evolves. It isn't something that can be taught, and there are no guidelines. You begin by training your dog, and one day you realize that you have spent over an hour working together and you have hardly spoken, yet you have had perfect communication. That's when you realize that you have something special. It doesn't mean that you won't make mistakes or that your dog won't at some point put the sheep through the wrong gate, but on the day you need your dog to be the best he can be – he will be. A dog's training, coupled with its instinct, tells it how to understand the sheep and when it needs to make a decision. The fine tuning of that training, coupled with a desire to please, makes the same dog a serious contender on the trials field. Not all collies will make this grade, and not all handlers are brilliant trainers, but a good handler will always get the best from his dog because it will always aim to please him. The following quote is from a sheepdog handler:

> I've seen a good dog ruined by a poor handler, and I've seen a less than average dog make the grade thanks to a good handler.

Mentors of the Past

I was lucky to be born on a farm and to grow up with collies, and I feel privileged to have been able to enter the world of shepherding and sheepdog handling. I am indebted to the shepherds who taught me so much: they were older and wiser than me, and had the knowledge of previous generations of shepherds who hadn't had the advantage of modern machinery and equipment. The knowledge that those wise men imparted will be passed down in their farming community, and if I can pass on just a little of that knowledge to those who today are outside farming but who love this breed, then I will feel that I have honoured those great mentors.

They had a wonderfully simple way of explaining things, and from the simplicity of their descriptions I learned that far too often we complicate things, when collies are actually uncomplicated. The commands used to train dogs for working sheep are simple: they need a left, a right, a stop, a walk on, and a recall. Most of the commands are universally in order: 'come by', 'away', 'lie down' or 'stand still', 'walk on', and 'that'll do'. They are rarely words or commands of one syllable, and the more lyrical the sound, the more a dog is able to detect it.

If you listen to the whistle commands given to dogs when they are working or competing at a sheepdog trial, you will find that, apart from the stop whistle, many of them echo bird sounds. The stop whistle is usually a shrill one-note whistle, but to me the one that really stands out is the 'that'll do' command. This is three words rolled into one, but different tones are used: one tone will be a recall, one will stop the dog from pushing a boundary, and one will calm a dog down. Dogs don't understand the actual words, they respond to the different pitches, and this would not work as well with just one syllable. We can teach a dog to 'sit', 'lie down' and 'stay', and it will understand the action we require for each word, but the simplicity of the shepherd and his dog is that of not having to teach so many different words when dogs love different tones. There is a down side to this as I once had a budgie imitate my whistles from his perch in the window, and he would counter command my dogs when I was training them.

Border Collies love to learn, they love to have a job to do, they love to be included, and they are brilliant team players. They are a free-spirited breed, and whether on a farm or in a companion home, as long as that spirit is allowed to develop, they will be happy dogs.

Summary

Border Collies are intelligent dogs and are able to make their own decisions when working sheep a great distance away from their handler. They are incredibly focused, and a well trained dog will remain calm even under pressure. They have been bred for different strengths, so their characters and personalities are not all the same. They are loyal, and although they love to work, they are also the masters of down time. As a breed, they are not used to being alone: even if working sheep as a single dog, their partner is the shepherd. In a home, they don't have to have another dog for company, but they do need guidance and someone they can trust.

CHAPTER 2

Sheepdog Trials

I was brought up with Border Collies. I have trained them for sheep work; I run a collie rescue; I rehabilitate problem dogs; and I have competed in sheepdog trials. I love the breed and have always had these amazing dogs in my life, but I still get a real surge of emotion when I watch a dog competing in one of the major sheepdog trials. There is something awesome about seeing a dog run almost half a mile to gather its sheep, then bring them halfway down the course and with one whistle from the handler, look back and gather more sheep from an entirely different direction. I am not ashamed to admit that I often watch with a lump in my throat.

Most of the work that a sheepdog does is behind the scenes. The picturesque scene of a dog gathering sheep on a hillside or moving sheep across a road from one field to another is usually the start, or the end, of the really hard work. Sheep are always being gathered or moved for a reason, and in addition to the gathering of the flock, a dog may need to drive the sheep into a pen, or to separate or 'shed' some of them from the rest of the flock. At some point it may have to think on its feet, taking the initiative without being told, and jump over a fence to head off and bring back a sheep trying to make an escape. Unless you are involved in the work this is rarely something you will see, but most of it is replicated on the course of a sheepdog trial.

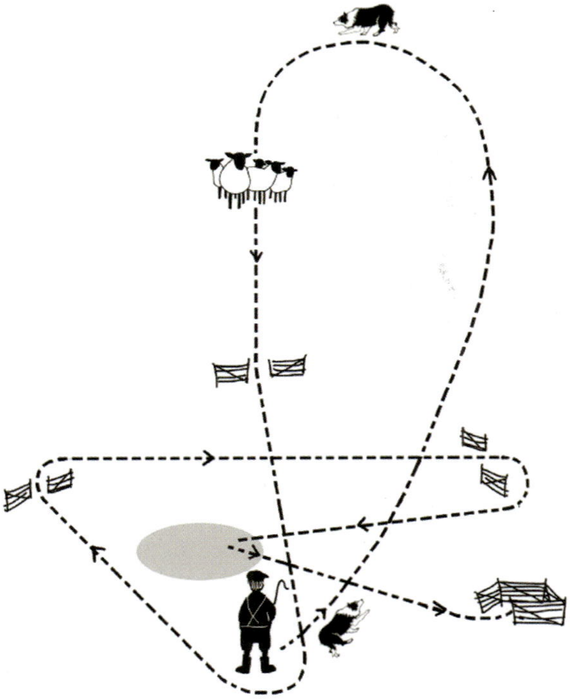

Trials are not all of the same standard, and winter is the usual time for nursery trials, for dogs that are competing for the first time. Ironically winter sheep are not always the best sheep for dogs to start on. They are usually young sheep and can often be unruly, also the ground often has little grass on it, and the weather can be cold and windy. Just like us, sheep can be affected by the weather, and I

Diagram of a trial course. The handler can choose to outrun his dog to the left or the right, but after that the course is set. This diagram shows a right-hand outrun, the fetch, a left-hand drive and through the last drive hurdle to the shedding ring and then to the pen. The handler remains at the post until the sheep enter the shedding ring.

This photo is taken from the bottom of the course, so you can see how far away the sheep are, just specks in the distance; from its position on the ground the dog will not be able to see the sheep.

remember an old shepherd telling me years ago, 'good keep (grass), good sheep; poor keep, poor sheep' – the theory being that with little grass on the ground there was nothing to slow the sheep down, but with a good covering of grass they would usually be steadier. But sheep often have their own agenda, and if they decide to take a nibble of that good grass they can make it very hard for the dog to keep them trotting round the course.

Summer is generally the season for open trials, for dogs that have passed the nursery standard; these are usually longer courses, and will often include a shed or a single – separating two or a single sheep from the others before or after the pen. Each part of the course is judged separately, and points awarded for each part.

The First Trials

The first recorded sheepdog trial in Wales was in Bala in 1873. A second trial followed in Scotland in Lanarkshire in 1874, and in 1876 a third was held in England in Alexandra Park in London. It's hard to imagine sheepdog trials being held in London now, but at one time they were held in Hyde Park from the 1930s to the 1960s. However, just as the Border Collie has a long history behind it, so trials have more background to them than is recorded.

Farmers and shepherds can be quite competitive about their dogs. If one man challenged another that his dog could gather sheep off the hills with the fewest whistles, and the other took up the challenge, suddenly there is a

Coming through the 'fetch' gates in a lovely straight line. Notice there is no sign of the dog: its power is such that it is often a distance from the sheep, but is still controlling them.

competition. I imagine this kind of rivalry would have opened the challenge to more handlers, and eventually to spectators, and in this way competitions would have been instigated long before recorded trials took place.

A sheepdog trial course is, ultimately, a test of a dog's ability to do the various jobs required of it when working sheep. Trials have changed very little over the years, apart from perhaps being a little more complicated, partly because a sheepdog's work is more involved now, but also there is far more competition than in the past so the courses are more testing.

The Trials Course

The Outrun

The outrun is probably the most important part of the course, as a poor outrun can unsettle the sheep, making them difficult to control. The dog needs to run out wide enough to be able go round the back of the sheep without upsetting them. Points can be deducted if a dog runs either too wide or too near to the sheep. Running too wide is usually when a dog runs along the fence, almost indicating it hasn't seen the sheep, whereas running too near, or 'tight', is when the dog doesn't go wide enough and the sheep can see the dog coming and often try to move away. Points are awarded or deducted at the judge's discretion, with much depending on how efficient the outrun is and how little it disturbs the sheep.

The Lift

The lift is when the dog comes in at the back of the sheep and 'lifts' them gently from a standing position to trot down the course. It sounds simple, but the sheep don't always stand politely waiting, and they don't always want to trot calmly forwards, and a dog has to learn to allow the sheep to move without following too closely. You can see how a poor outrun can subsequently spoil the lift.

The Fetch

The fetch used to be, and I believe still is at some hill trials, the straightest line from lifting the sheep to the handler. Most trials now have the sheep held at the top of the course, positioned in as straight a line as possible to the handler, with a set of hurdles (the fetch gates) halfway down the fetch, to be negotiated by the sheep – not necessarily the dog.

The Drive

When the sheep reach the bottom of the course the dog must take them in as tight a turn as possible round the handler and then start to drive them away towards the first drive gate. Once they are through that hurdle they make a tight turn again and start the 'cross drive' to the last hurdle, where they make another tight turn back to the handler. During this time the handler cannot leave his position at the bottom of the course.

In the majority of trials the next task is to put the sheep in a pen, and once the sheep have turned from the last hurdle the handler can then go to the pen and open the gate ready for them.

If a shepherd can see the sides of his sheep as they trot on the 'cross drive' he will know they are on line for the last drive hurdle. The sheep with a red collar are the ones to be shed or singled in the shedding ring.

The last drive hurdle, and the dog is just out of sight on the left; he will need to run very fast and very wide to make the tight turn needed to score points.

The dog is closing in to make sure the sheep go into the pen and not down the side of it.

Shed and Single

Shedding is separating two sheep or one single sheep from the rest. There is usually a designated area where this must take place, and often a 'shedding' ring is marked out on the ground, usually with sawdust. Although the dog can leave the ring in order to accomplish this task, any sheep that leave the ring will mean the handler will lose some points.

Trials and Tribulations

When I first began competing I was told that a triallist needed the sheep, the dog and the weather all to be perfect at the same time, and if they were, then the handler would often panic and make a mistake. I found out how true this was on several occasions. It's one thing making mistakes in winter at the nursery or novice trials, but competing in an open trial and watching your packet of sheep invade the judge's tent, assisted by your ever faithful sheepdog, is no joke. I know this as my dog, Meg, was brilliant at waiting for a big trial and then invading the judge's space, or the beer tent, with her sheep. We all have to start somewhere, and by the end of our first competitive season she began to understand that only the course was for her and the sheep. The judge's space was to be kept clear of so as not to cause any bad feeling, and the beer tent was for me to get over the shock of a good run. It took a lot of time and patience, and quite a few embar-

rassing moments, but from four years old she seemed to decide to go easy on me, and together we competed at national and international level.

These dogs are truly amazing when you think that many of them are working large flocks of sheep, are given very few commands from their handlers, and often make their own decisions. Yet they go on to the trials field and are told what to do and when to do it, as they work hard to take sheep through gateways with no fences on either side, and put sheep into a pen, only for their handler to let them straight back out again.

Not all dogs are able to compete, not because they can't, but because they simply don't want to. They can be brilliant working dogs, but that doesn't automatically qualify them to be good trialling dogs, and it shouldn't matter. It's important that a working dog can work sheep, but competing in sheepdog trials is a bonus. If a dog is trained specifically to be a good trial dog it will have no real work experience – this will be evident at a big competition, which is a replica of all working tasks. However, a dog that is a good working dog will always have the capability to complete a trials course, though not necessarily to the standard needed to gain any points from the judges.

I believe it is important to listen to what our dogs have to say. They may not speak our language, but that doesn't mean they can't communicate with us. A term I often hear, and one that I really object to, is when a collie is described as a 'failed sheepdog'. I don't believe there is any such thing. If a dog can't or won't work sheep it is

Max and Sheepdog Trials

Max was an amazing working dog. He needed very little training and always seemed to know what I needed him to do – until it came to a trials course. He would try to bring all the sheep out of the holding pen; he would run a perfect course; and then just before the finish he would jump a fence and gather a flock of sheep in another field. Time and again I told people what an amazing dog he was, and then one lovely shepherd said to me, 'When are you going to listen to him? He wants to work, he wants to please you, but he sees no point in what he has to do on a trials field – listen to your dog!' Happiness is more important than competing. Max had the capability to be a great trials dog, but it didn't make him happy. He went on to earn me a living shepherding and training young dogs for other shepherds. He was a legend in his own right and a wonderful friend.

either lacking in its breeding – rare, but possible – or it has been taken to sheep before it was ready to start training, or the handler simply didn't know how to train it. The 'failure' can be one of many things, but it should never be a dog's label.

Training Young Dogs

There is nothing unusual about a shepherd or farmer not being able to train his own dog. Going back in their history we can see how the shepherds and their dogs practically lived together, and training would be a matter of learning just a little bit more every day. But in our much faster modern world, farmers don't always have the time to train their own dogs. In some cases they will have bought dogs already trained, and then one day they have a pup and are faced with the basics which they haven't done before – plus their job might not allow them the much needed time to learn and to train. In those instances it is better for the dog to go to someone who has the time and the knowledge to teach the youngster its basics so it can go back home ready for 'work experience'.

It may seem harsh sending a dog away for what is usually an eight-week period, but it is little different to

The dog is closing in to make sure the sheep go into the pen and not down the side of it.

a dog going to a boarding kennels when the owner is on holiday. My daughter Vicki takes in dogs for training, and sometimes I think that if the dog could cook a meal some of the farmers would rather send their wives in for training! They are on their mobile phones every other day asking if their dog is all right – little knowing that after a week of settling in, their dog is happily learning to work sheep and is enjoying itself. Until of course the day they are reunited, when Vicki has to ask the owner to sneak quietly up the track so they can see their dog working before it smells them. And I do mean smell them: it will be working, and every so often it will slow down and sniff the air. And when Vicki calls it off the sheep it knows exactly where to run to find its owner, and then it's a grand reunion.

Whether a dog is going to be solely a working dog, or the handler has aspirations for it to be a trial dog, it's important that its first experience of working sheep is a positive one. It takes a long time to train a dog to work, and for trialling there has to be more precision. Taking a few extra strides before stopping at the back of the sheep on a trials course can determine a good run or a bad one, whereas at the back of a flock of sheep a dog will rarely need to stop at all.

The dog's keen sense of smell and hearing can be very distracting for it when it is competing, especially at summer trials where there can be refreshment tents, other dogs and of course picnics. But if we refer back to Chapter 1, when we discussed a dog's amazing ability to focus, we can understand how all the things that might in theory excite a dog aren't even noticed by it – until after its run and you notice that your picnic sausage rolls are missing!

The Competition

Watching a sheepdog trial may not be something on your list of things to do. If you have been a spectator at a winter or a small summer trial I can understand that it may have seemed as if it would only be of interest to the competitors. However, I would recommend that if possible you go to a national or international trial – the latter being the ultimate, with the final day being the supreme championship, which includes a double lift (gathering two separate groups of sheep) and taking all twenty sheep round a very large and testing course.

I could describe the whole event, but it really has to be seen to be appreciated, and I don't think anyone could fail to be impressed by the dogs and their behaviour. They are usually only on a lead immediately prior to competing, and you will see groups of competitors catching up and discussing the price of sheep and lambs, and whose dog is tipped to do well. Their dogs will be quietly watching the current run, and I can sit and watch them for hours as they patiently wait their turn to compete, their heads bobbing from side to side as people stand in front of them and block their view.

For me it isn't just about the competition, it's about the atmosphere. There is a calmness about the dogs and handlers, and everything seems to run so smoothly – but the amount of work setting up the course is tremendous. For example, if the outrun has a designated distance then it must be accurate, as must the distance between the hurdles. Furthermore if you are present at the start or end of a trial you may just see the handlers and their dogs unwittingly creating a scene that would make a brilliant cartoon. It is the responsibility of the farmers and shepherds to build and/or dismantle the course, and where one minute they are smartly dressed, suddenly they appear in working clothes and on their quad bikes, doing whatever is their designated job at a speed that could instil fear into even the most hardened driver of fast cars.

But even more impressive is that as they lean over the handlebars, a collie will be seen balancing on the back of the bike (they only seem to lie down when it is stationary), standing with face to the wind, tongue out and a huge 'grin' on its face. This is handler and dog doing what they do best – the competition is over, so back to work. These dogs may not have a designer bed, live in a centrally heated home or go on long holidays, but they are ecstatically happy. As long as the person they are working with understands them, they will get dirty, they will probably learn a few choice words, and they will quickly learn that jumping over a hurdle into a sheep pen and showering your human with sheep excrement (yes, I've had that done to me!) is best not done.

A sheepdog trial is a competition, and every competitor will at some point dream of that ultimate win, the one that brings recognition and says 'my dog is a great dog'. But it's also about the camaraderie, the catching up with old friends, and making new ones. It's about the chit chat in the refreshment tent, about whose dog did what, and it's an insight into the everyday tasks that a working dog takes in its stride.

Summary

A sheepdog trials course is designed to test dogs on as many aspects of working sheep as possible, but being a good worker doesn't necessarily mean that a dog can come up with the precision needed to trial. Not all winners on the trials field come from trialling stock. My own dog Meg was a well bred dog, yet although none of her immediate ancestors had competed, she was in both national and international trials. A good working dog will not chase or attack sheep, and is happy riding on a tractor or chilling out on a bale of straw when the work is done.

Collies trained to work sheep and to compete in sheepdog trials can be working hard and to precision, but they also know how to switch off and be calm. Their work isn't just physical; when at a distance from the shepherd, their job can involve making decisions about a problem sheep that the shepherd hasn't noticed.

CHAPTER 3

Colour Genes and Character

There is a saying, 'Don't judge a book by its cover' (meaning that first appearances can be misleading), but if there is a picture on the cover it will give some indication of what is inside the book. We need to look at each Border Collie as an individual and not just as a breed, because a dog's physical appearance (or its 'cover') can tell us such a lot about its character. Collies can be long- or short-coated, black and white, tri-coloured, merles, and a variety of colour mixtures. They don't all have the same colour eyes, and eyes can be the key to understanding certain behaviours, and to solving some problems. But first we need to understand why there is such a variety, and how it can often be the key to help us understand them.

With someone we know we can usually judge what their reaction may be in certain circumstances. It's not as easy with someone we don't know, but we can sometimes have a good idea – and this is not because of their clothes or their job, it is more about their attitude and their body language. So it is equally exciting that with knowledge of the different colour genes and the breed characteristics, not only will you be able to 'read' your own dog, but you will know how to react to a friend's or even a stranger's collie.

A short-coated, tri-coloured, amber-eyed, prick-eared collie will have a different character to a similar coloured dog but with brown eyes, and it will be different again if the ears are dropped or the coat is black and white. Not only do these dogs differ in character, but their energy levels, sensitivity and their reaction to other dogs and people can be different. For me, this is one of the most intriguing things about the breed. With knowledge of their inherited genes, training can be managed according to their individual traits – helping to make them well adjusted dogs with few problems. Of course there are going to be some problems. I think the perfect child or dog is yet to be found, and if they were, I believe they'd be rather boring. But problems need solutions, and whilst our own dogs are perfect to us, deep down we all know that at some point we've had to sit and think, 'I didn't see that coming'; but with a bit more background on each one, you stand a better chance of seeing it coming. They will still be just as special, but you will be one jump ahead.

Instinct and Behaviour

To understand how resourceful collies are, we can compare them to ourselves and our work. In a company a team of people will work together, balancing strengths. One member of the team may be brilliant at sales but not as confident in advertising, while the one who is good at advertising may not be as strong in the technical department. The larger the team the more varied the strengths, and the larger the company the more teams there will be specializing in different sectors of that company.

Then we have the sole trader who becomes the 'Jack of all trades'. This person can do the accounts, the sales and the advertising, and although there is usually a department that they don't excel at, they are still capable of running a very good business. Finally we have the sole trader who really has rather too much work to do and would benefit from employing someone, but holds back because time is needed to train the new employee, and there is also the question of whether the business can afford the extra expense…

Now back to our collies, and the more sheep the shep-

Tri-coloured, hazel eyes, soft features and gentle ears denote a nice-natured collie and one eager to please.

Tri-coloured and hazel eyes, but a richer brown and upright ears: this is usually a dog that can get wound up quite easily, doesn't like certain people in its space, and can be stubborn.

The strong amber eye is focused, but this tri-coloured collie has a medium-length coat, and his ears don't prick straight up. Although focused, he will be sensitive. If he had a short coat and pricked up ears he would probably not like strangers or children in his space.

herd has, the more dogs he will need – whereas the shepherd with a small flock of perhaps 200 sheep may only need one dog: the Jack of all trades. If he expands his flock he is asking a lot of one dog, and then he has three choices: find the time to train a second dog; pay a lot of money for a fully trained dog; or carry on as he is, and risk his one dog being overworked.

We know from the two previous chapters that Border Collies have evolved from droving, to working, to the élite dog we know today, by virtue of very careful and selective breeding. However, it will never have been as simple as breeding a dog just to be able to work sheep, as a sheepdog has to have many different skills, and they rarely, if ever, all come together in just one dog. A dog that has a really good outrun may not be as good at driving sheep away, and the strong driving dog may have what shepherds call an 'economic' outrun, meaning that it will not run out wide enough to avoid upsetting the sheep.

Each dog will have different instincts. A shepherd with a large flock of sheep may take his 'gathering' dogs to gather the whole flock, and as they get closer he may send out the 'driving' dogs as back-up. Taking them back he will use his 'driving' dog, or dogs, and his 'gather-

The amber eye again, but on a black-and-white dog with a longer, soft coat and ears that don't prick full up. Both this dog's parents were long coated with hazel eyes, so the amber eye was a throwback gene. A gentle, calm dog with a nice nature.

This could almost be the same dog as the previous photograph, but it isn't. Her eyes are a softer hazel colour, her ears do not prick up as much, and her body is stockier. Capable of being really calm, but will be excitable.

Black and white with a light eye and prick ears, but not as pricked as some, and a medium coat. Sensitive and not happy in new situations or with new people.

Another variety of black-and-white: this dog has gentle, half-pricked ears, a rich hazel eye, and a medium coat; she has black-and-white parents but a tri-coloured grandparent. She has a lovely, gentle nature; she doesn't look for trouble, and is not overly brave.

'ing' dogs will be back-up. Any of those dogs may have a 'strong eye' and can hypnotize a sheep with its stare, literally keeping it still until the shepherd is close enough to catch it. The dog with a very strong eye is rarely the best 'gathering' dog, as its instinct is to stalk, and it will 'hold' one sheep with its gaze.

We can take from this that the collie is a good team player, but we also need to remember that the shepherd is part of that team. A dog never works totally alone: it can work without other dogs, but its day will centre round the shepherd. This is something we can take forward with us for the chapters on its needs in a companion home.

Colour and Coat Texture

You are probably thinking that the colour and texture of a coat can't make a difference to how a dog behaves, and you will be right. But it isn't the coat, it's the genes that are behind the coat. We all resemble someone in our gene pool, and the chances are that if we look like them, we also share some of their traits. Going back to the third paragraph in Chapter 1, I do resemble my paternal grandmother, though I'm not sure how much I appreciate her genes, as she was determined, feisty, not to be argued with, and quite hard in her attitude to her children. But I also inherited some of my maternal grandmother's genes, and they were gentler, not as demanding, and very kind. Life has made me use every bit of strength and determination I had, but I was never hard with my children, and for that I have my mother to thank – who taught me how to manage my inherited traits and how to keep them balanced. In the same way, managing a collie's genes and character is about balance.

Let us take a look at some of the inherited traits of the Border Collie, and their purpose. If the shepherd's dog will be working all the year round and in all weathers, his choice will be for a dog whose coat doesn't get tangled or take ages to dry, and if that same dog will be working on the hills and in strong winds he wants to know it can hear him. So we are now looking at a short-coated, prick-eared dog, bred to run great distances over rough ground and in all weather conditions, and with acute hearing. This will be a dog with a lot of stamina and very noise sensitive.

Once a dog like this is proving how well it can work, it will be paired with a dog that has compatible gene lines, and should the dog be the same colour, then that colour will carry the genes through to the progeny. If one dog is tri-coloured and the other is black and white, then the inherited genes from each colour will pass down the line. Dogs with slightly longer coats are more likely to have been employed for 'in-bye' work, such as in valleys and enclosed fields. Dogs with longer coats and dropped tips to their ears will still have very keen hearing, but often not as finely tuned as shorter-coated dogs.

Examples of Inherited Colour Genes

Laddie was tri-coloured with a medium coat, his ear tips dropped over, and he had a sturdy body. Meg was black and white with a medium coat, pricked ears, and a fine-boned frame. A union with them produced a mixture of colours and type. The short-coated, tri-coloured, prick-eared pups made strong dogs and needed experienced handlers. The black-and-white, strong-bodied ones were stubborn, and the black-and-white, fine-boned dogs were sensitive. The dogs that resembled their parents and grandparents in colour, also inherited some of their characteristics.

It's rather like a jigsaw: once you have all the pieces and start putting them into place, you begin to see the picture. Laddie's tri-coloured mum had a tri-coloured grandfather, who was a strong, confident dog. Laddie's father was black-and-white and calm, but his father was another strong, tri-coloured, prick-eared dog. Meg's mother was black-and-white and short-coated, and her father was black-and-white with a long coat and pricked ears. Meg's line went back to Wiston Cap, and most of her ancestors were sensitive, prick-eared dogs, with only a few carrying a tri-coloured gene. If this sounds confusing, try going over the paragraph again and split it into first Laddie and then Meg, and you will start to see the picture forming of how the strong tri-coloured gene, blended with the more sensitive genes of Meg, produced well balanced dogs with different qualities.

Now you are probably asking the question 'why bother, why not breed like to like?' If we breed like to like, not only will we lose some important qualities, but we will cause problems. Breeding Meg to a similar line of her own characteristics would have resulted in oversensitive, very highly strung collies, and breeding Laddie to a similar line of his own would have produced some very dominant dogs, which, if not handled correctly, could become belligerent. The Border Collie is an amazing breed: it is intelligent, sensitive, strong and gentle, loyal, faithful, hard working and a wonderful companion. To make sure that those qualities don't get lost or weakened, any breeding must be for compatibility and balance.

Another question I often hear is, 'Does is matter, do we need all those qualities in a companion dog?' But I can't think why we wouldn't want those qualities, as they are the essence of the Border Collie: what we don't want is a dog that has lost some of those positive qualities by having too many negatives ones.

Balanced Breeding

Many years ago I was waiting for my run at a sheepdog trial, and while watching another dog competing, I asked a friend what would happen if I put Meg to that particular dog, my reasoning being that Meg's only shortcoming was driving sheep away, and the dog on the course was a brilliant driving dog. His response was instant: 'You can only have so many genes in the pool, lass, so do it and you may get a dog that can drive sheep from here to London, but don't come crying to me when you discover it can't outrun, or its temperament is lacking.' I fully understood what he was saying, and it really drilled home to me the importance of balanced breeding.

Different coat lengths, textures and colours, and how the ears are set, can give an indication of a dog's char-

acter, and also of any traits that may have been passed down the ancestral line. The further back you can go on that line, the more information you will have – or as I often say, the more pieces you will have acquired for your jigsaw. Laddie's strong and often stubborn gene was inherited not just from his father but also from his grandfather, a double dose of stubbornness quite near to him in his line. The tri-coloured gene is often a strong gene, and if it goes with a short coat it may take precedence over a milder gene. For example, a pup may have two black-and-white parents, but if one of the grandparents were tri-coloured, there is a chance that the puppy will inherit some of that dog's traits, especially if it is short-coated. If you don't see the parents but other pups in the litter are tri-coloured, then you can assume that your black-and-white one is carrying the tri-coloured gene.

My intention in this book is not to baffle you with technical terms – for example, if I use words such as 'chromosome', 'recessive genes' and 'homozygous' you will either know exactly what I mean, or you will decide it's far too complicated and put the book down. I don't do complicated, and I don't want you to think that you need to if you are to understand the different jigsaw pieces of our breed. It's fun, and if you can grasp the fun side of it you will enjoy meeting all the different collie characters in your life and 'reading' them.

Some tri-coloured collies can be stubborn, and the shorter-coated, prick-eared ones can be super sensitive. Merles are usually 'busy' dogs, always wanting to be on the go, and are often too busy to have an agenda. Red dogs can be very high-energy dogs – though don't mistake brown for red. Short-coated dogs are often more highly strung than those with a longer coat, and small, fine-boned dogs are usually very sensitive. This a good guide, and in most cases will be accurate – but there is always the exception to the rule. However, you can usually look back into the ancestry of the 'exception', and find that the jigsaw pieces you find, once put together, would produce the dog that you thought was an exception.

Border Collie Eyes

The eyes of a collie can tell you a lot about them, their temperament, their difficulties, their fears, and their feelings about other dogs and people. I don't use the term

Red-and-white dogs have just as much variety in their character as black-and-white and tri-coloured dogs. This girl has amber eyes, but her body is of stocky build, her coat is medium, and her ears do not prick up. She has the sensitive high-energy gene of the red, but her nature is gentle although excitable.

A different type of red, with amber eyes and really pricked-up ears. She has a high energy level, is always busy, is sensitive, and doesn't like strangers in her space.

Fight or Flight Distance

The 'fight or flight' distance is the distance between sheep and dog at the point where the sheep decides whether to stand its ground, or to move away. We understand this as our personal space – for the sheepdog it's the distance from a sheep that a dog with a strong eye will choose to stand and 'eye' it; it is also the distance from a group of sheep that a dog needs in order to move them without upsetting them. While the dog is outside the perimetre of the sheep's 'fight or flight' distance, the sheep will turn and move away, taking the 'flight' choice. On the edge of that distance the sheep will turn to face the dog, but will not make the decision to 'fight' unless the dog moves in, which it shouldn't do – and there we have the stand-off, allowing time for the shepherd to catch the sheep.

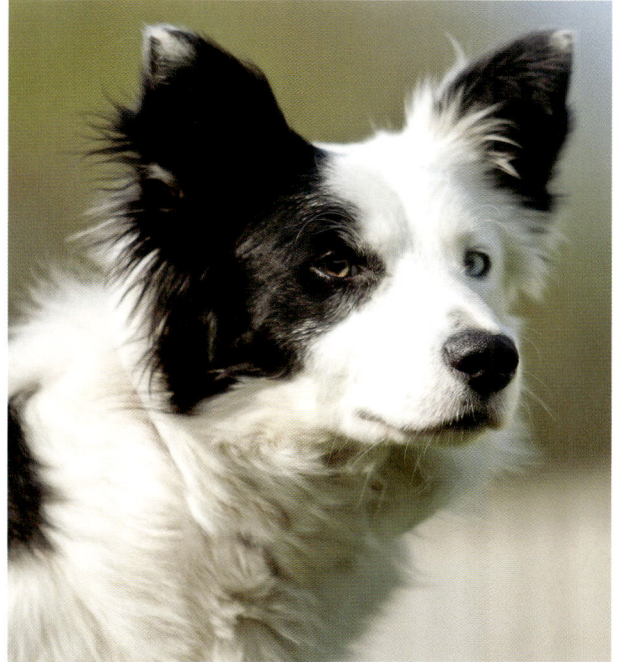

This boy is black and white, his ears stand up but don't prick up, he has a light hazel eye and a wall eye. His half-white face will be with the wall-eyed gene, he has high energy levels, a mind of his own, and is probably choosy about whom he likes.

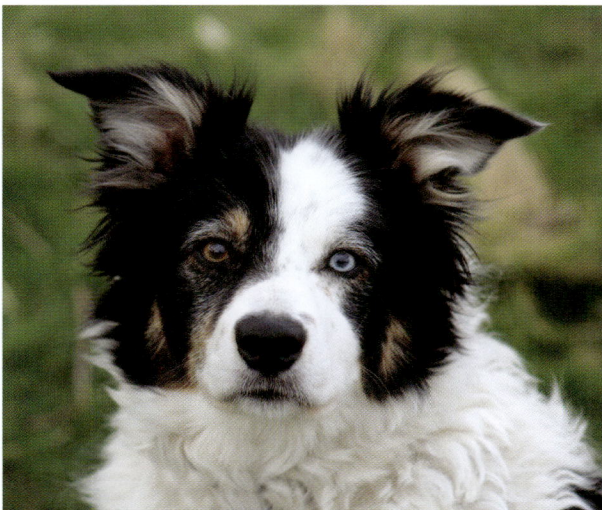

Tri-coloured and a blue eye but soft ears, a longer coat than the dog in the previous photograph and a stocky body, sensitive and excitable, maybe even rather temperamental, but nice natured.

'collie eye', as it is often used to describe a problem when in fact the eye can be a key to preventing problems. Not all collies have the same eye power, nor do they all have the same colour of eyes, which can be amber, hazel, brown, dark brown, or blue (wall eye). A wall eye is the result of a merle gene that can skip several generations and then suddenly appear again, often only in just one or two of a litter.

A very dark brown eye is rarely a collie with working instincts as the eye is too dark, or is not hypnotic enough, to 'hold' a sheep still with its gaze. The brown- and hazel-eyed dogs are usually good all-round dogs; in the work situation they can gather, drive sheep away, and the hazel eyes can 'hold' a sheep still until the shepherd is near enough to catch it. The amber-eyed dog has all the power needed to hypnotize a sheep, and it will often single out a sheep to stare at it. These dogs don't like people in their space.

I have explained this as simply as I can, and as we go through the book you will see how valuable this

Working out the character of different collies is fun and it is also like reading the introduction to a book. The colour and set of the body will tell you what to expect and how to manage it. Tri-coloured with short to medium coat and dropped tipped years says, 'I am full of energy, sensitive and will try and push the boundaries but once I understand them I will respect them'. But there is also a blue fleck in this dog's eye, which means she will challenge what she believes to be a wrong decision.

information is in managing the different characters and their traits. As a rule the lighter the eye, the more power a dog will have, and the more power it has, the greater the 'fight or flight' distance.

We mustn't mistake power for dominance, nor should we think that a collie with the power to stand up to a stubborn sheep is aggressive. It's about understanding each dog as an individual, and then managing it. Dogs are surrendered to a rescue centre when they have been mismanaged, when their characters have not been understood – and through lack of knowledge of the breed's negative behaviours, these behaviours have almost been encouraged, resulting in a confused and misunderstood dog that has to be rehomed.

Summary

The coat colour and set of the body is a good indicator of a dog's character. Understanding the different characters and instincts will make it easier to train a dog, and will help in managing its instincts. Some are naturally strong minded, and all are sensitive, but some more than others. Brown-eyed dogs may welcome eye contact, but the lighter-eyed dogs will want to keep their distance from strangers. However, there are always exceptions to any rule, and each dog is the result of the compatibility of its breeding, and how well it is understood.

PART TWO

The Border Collie in your Home

CHAPTER 4

The Companion Border Collie

We have looked at the collie as the 'shepherd's working companion' in both its working life and its competitive life, but now we're going to look at it as a companion in the home. How does the dog that is bred to work, and whose instincts are honed for working, manage without the job he was bred to do? How can he employ his intelligence without the problem-solving tasks that he is faced with when working sheep? How will he cope with a life

Dogs love to clean themselves by rolling, and for them it's great for back scratching.

Collies do like company, and if they get on well with each other it's lovely for them to have a friend…

…but you don't have to get another dog to keep the first one company. Sometimes all they need is to know you are always there for them, and you can be your dog's best friend and companion.

that doesn't use a fraction of the energy that he is capable of producing? The answers begin in the first three chapters. We need to understand how he used his instincts for work and why, we need to have a good idea which type of colour gene he is carrying, and what the strengths are – and then we manage them, in the same way that we would manage a five-year-old child. We understand, we empathize and we teach.

There are many misconceptions connected to the breed and its instincts. One of the big questions is: should a collie live in a companion home? Few dogs will live inside when they are working. Unlike the farmer, they aren't able to take a shower every evening, and even if the farmer may not want one, if he smells of all things unsavoury he might have to have one or risk not getting his evening meal! Dogs don't usually like having to be bathed; they prefer to roll in some clean straw or long grass. Nevertheless, quite a lot of farm dogs retire into the farm home, or are retired to a local home.

So by going to the source, we know that they are adaptable, they love to work, and equally, they love to chill out. Some may like a cosy bed and some may prefer a hard floor, but as long as they are with someone, they will be happy. We also know that if we study the colour genes, some will settle better into certain environments than others.

Collies with Children

Collies round children up and will nip them because that's what they do with sheep. Really? They don't know the difference between sheep and little humans? They may appear to round them up, and they may nip them, but only as they would play with other dogs, and in particular, with their littermates. In the dog world, nipping can be an acceptable part of play – but they shouldn't do it with children. Collies like to control movement, but they don't have to: it's about managing their instincts and knowing which instincts are prevalent in your dog. We will go into more detail about collies and children in Chapter 11.

Collies love to be with someone, and if left regularly for long periods of time they can become bored and destructive – and adding another dog for company can sometimes cause more problems. Two dogs that bond will play, but they may become destructive, and will probably form a relationship that doesn't include closeness with their

guardian. If two dogs don't bond, then you may need to keep them separate because they are fighting. Dogs need parenting and guidance, and they need boundaries. Bonding to another dog and excluding their guardian, or an uncomfortable or aggressive dog-to-dog relationship, are both situations that won't materialize if the dogs are parented. Having two dogs because someone wants two dogs is fine, but getting another dog to keep the first one happy is rarely a good solution.

Dogs need company, but they don't have to be interacting with that company all the time. If someone is working from home, maybe sitting at a desk, the dog has someone to be with and someone to feel safe with. Our previous chapters tell us this breed is not a loner, it's a team player, and it loves companionship.

As a companion they ask for very little, and sometimes they can be overwhelmed with too much too soon. They are used to amusing themselves – as puppies they will find things to play with and they will invent their own games. As they grow up they are still capable of entertaining themselves, but humans often take away that simple pleasure, because they want them to have the best. I know when my children were little they were given a Christmas present in a huge box: the present got a whoop of excitement, and then they spent the rest of the day inventing games to play with the box. It was a very expensive gift and the expression on the face of the person who gave it to them is something I will remember forever. It was a real lesson in how children can amuse themselves without spending a fortune.

I always maintain that having a collie is like permanently taking care of a five-year-old child. Good manners, respect, fun, teaching and learning together. Are you prepared for a five-year-old in your life?

Expectations

Before getting a collie I think everyone should ask themselves an important question: 'Why do I want a collie, and what do I expect from it?' It's one thing wanting one, but sometimes the time or the circumstances just aren't right, and if they aren't right, no matter how much you would love one, it's better to wait. It's not just about our expectations: it's about the dog, and what *it* needs and expects. If we look at the life of the collie in the past, his needs were very simple, and although *our* lives have changed over the centuries, collies and *their* needs have

Short-coated dogs are often more susceptible to stress, and if other factors are added, such as tri-colour and light eyes, such a dog often cannot cope and becomes very stressed.

changed very little. Where we have dreams and ambitions, work and schedules, their requirements are more straightforward: they need their own place to sleep, a good meal, companionship and a job.

Remember we are talking about the dog's basic needs before going into a home. He needs somewhere he can feel safe enough to sleep, and he needs food because without it he cannot survive. If dogs were free to roam and were not dependent on humans, their work would be to

hunt for food, and they would be free to seek their own companionship.

The same might be said for all dogs, but we are looking at a breed whose natural instincts need nurturing, not confining in order to be at its best, and if we can provide the physical needs, we are also creating an empathy with its emotional needs. However, when we take these dogs into our lives and our homes, we make their choices for them – what they can eat and when, where and when to

A collie doesn't have to be doing something all the time. A farm dog will stand for a long time patiently watching sheep. He will watch every sheep that moves to see where it goes and what it does, and although his body will be motionless, his mind will be alert and working.

A blue merle with two blue eyes. Merles are usually very sensitive and always love to be doing something. This dog is unlike a tri-merle as he has no brown on him, and the longer coat is a hint that he will not always be in 'overdrive', but he has pricked ears so he will be sensitive to noise.

exercise – and although they may be free to choose which other dogs they do or don't associate with, they are not free to choose their lifelong companion. We do that for them when we take them into our lives.

The collie's expectations are quite simple, yet you will find a lot of advice about the collie in your home which is complicated. They really don't have to be 'doing' all the time, and they don't need to be kept mentally stimulated all the time. Remember the five-year-old child parallel, and think about how you would probably spend a lot of time trying to keep the child calm, and avoiding things that over-excite them. Of course your collie needs exercise, but it doesn't have to run for miles every day – and yes, it needs mental stimulation, but not all day, and again not if it causes over-excitement. The short-coated, tri-coloured dogs with pricked-up ears are a real candidate for getting over-exited, which is often accompanied by stress.

A dog on a farm is not working all the time, and when he is, he will be thinking and working out how best to do his job, so he is using both body and brain. When he's not working he will either be with the shepherd who is his companion, or he will be in his pen having some 'down time'. His pen may be a barn, a dog run, a stable or a kennel, or he may be tied up. His needs are thus pretty much covered, and without any complicated or expensive extras.

I abhor any kind of cruelty, be it mental or physical, and sadly it goes on in both pet and farm homes. In both cases these people are not animal lovers, and in my humble opinion should not be allowed near animals. However, we must not mistake common sense for cruelty. Sometimes a dog on a farm may be tied up to prevent it from deciding to go walkabout and to round up sheep without permission. No matter how good a dog may be with sheep, until it grows up it can be a danger to livestock. A good shepherd will revere his dog, and as previously stated in Chapter 3, many shepherds would rather lose contact with their partner than with their dog. But it is wrong for a dog to be tied up for the whole of every day and night.

In just the same way some may consider that the companion dog doesn't have a very good life if it is not participating in any of the dog disciplines, or isn't going out for a ten-mile hike each day – but if it is loved, has normal exercise, and is blessed with companionship, it will be a happy dog. But to have a dog in a home and *not* meet its needs of exercise and companionship is no different to the person who keeps a dog tied up all the time. If you decide you want to do agility or obedience, if you want to go to training classes, or if you prefer just to go walking and to enjoy your dog, it is your choice.

But remember that your dog doesn't have a choice, so make sure that whatever path you choose you are doing it for the right reasons, and not just because it's something *you've* always wanted to do. You don't have to do any of those for your dog to be using his brain; there are many ways you can give your dog a job of work to do without having to compete or join a class. This breed of dog loves to work with you, and isn't interested in who else is there or who is watching.

I think that some people who have a companion collie sometimes feel guilty because they feel it should be working, and they have prevented it from doing what it would love to do. I know this is true of some people who have come to me for help with their collie, and their feelings of guilt have often come from someone who has told them they were wrong to have a 'working' collie in their home. A division has been made between a farm home and a companion home – but we cannot divide the breed. It is a working breed, it is bred to work and has working instincts, and if it doesn't have those instincts then it isn't the collie we know and love. The wonderful thing about this breed is how adaptable it is, and how willing it is to try and please us – but if it has been bred to lose that working instinct, then it is no longer the dog that has been bred for generations to be our companion as well as a working dog.

The Collie in the Home

I have always maintained that a collie is not a difficult dog to understand, and if you understand them they are easy to live with – but young or old, they will keep you on your toes! If you take a puppy into your home you can have a few months of lovely puppyhood, then several months of adolescent dog, and finally from two years onwards your young companion will start to be an adult. There are going to be teething troubles, as with any breed of dog, but it should be a fun learning time for you both. However, if the boundaries are not made clear to your pup it might become an adolescent or an adult with 'attitude'. You need to be prepared for each stage of growth, and the changes in your dog as it reaches each stage. Later we will go through the ways of how to nurture a puppy while

All puppies are lovely, but they will not all be the same as they grow up. This little pup with his half white face and one blue eye will soon be pushing the boundaries.

guiding him or her to be a sensible adult dog.

To understand a collie you need to get inside his head and see the world through his eyes. When he comes into your home, be it as a puppy, an older dog or a rescue, what he sees and does will stay with him. An incident in a child's formative years can leave an impression that lasts a long time without them realizing it. My mum used to take me to a local outdoor paddling pool, and tried every method imaginable to get me in that pool, but something had upset me and the more she tried, the more I fought her. As a result I had a fear of learning to swim, which I didn't overcome until I was in my late teens, and to this day I'm wary of deep water. If my mum had left the idea alone for a while there was a good chance that things would have been different, but she wasn't to know that, and I only figured it out as I learned more about dogs.

A Good Guardian

Being a sensible guardian for a dog means teaching it good manners and respect, just as we would educate a young child. You can describe your position in your dog's life with any words you choose: pack leader, parent figure, the boss, the leader, even top dog if you prefer. They are simply words, and as long as you don't become a harsh teacher, and you strive to be a good guardian and companion, then your relationship is between you and your dog.

47

A well behaved collie is a joy to live with, and it is worth all the time, patience and hard work that is needed for that end result.

The first few days in your home for your dog are very much the same as the young child, even for an older dog, as it's a new beginning and anything that happens to please or upset him can set a pattern for the future; therefore it's important that you keep your home calm, and don't overload your new compan-ion with too much information. Those first few days are the time you need to lay the precious foundation stones for your relationship.

If you were entering a home with people who were strangers, how would you feel and behave? As a child you would be nervous, but you would welcome some guid-

Nell

Nell was a puppy when she went to her new home, and the first two days she spent most of her time in the garden, playing and bonding with her guardian. On the third day she ran into the kitchen and squatted down to urinate on the floor: in a moment of panic her guardian shouted '*No!*' and leaned forward to pick Nell up mid-flow. Nell ran out of the house, and no amount of coaxing could get her to go back to her guardian. It was a simple mistake made by someone who loved her pup – but the suddenness of the act, coupled with the pup's temperament, caused a serious issue.

If we look at the problem above from Nell's point of view she had spent two days playing, her guardian had encouraged her to have lots of fun, and she had become over-excited. She couldn't help the urge to relieve herself, and the sudden outburst from someone whom she thought of as a playmate was a shock to her. Had her guardian guided the play more and realized that Nell was becoming over-excited the situation could have been avoided.

ance, some gentle parenting to make you feel safe. As an adult you would be curious, and if you were a nervous person you might feel you just wanted to go to your room and stay there. But if you were more outward-going you might want to explore and maybe take just a few liberties, helping yourself to a glass of water or a biscuit: this might go unrecognized, or it might be ignored, but it does set you on your way to helping yourself.

Before making any decision about a collie's behaviour we need to look at the world from its point of view, and once we can see life from its perspective, it can help us to problem solve.

Summary

A good home isn't about bricks and mortar: it doesn't matter if a collie is on a farm and working, or in a companion home. It's about love and understanding, and giving a dog what it needs, rather than what we think it should have. We also need to be aware that we can't provide the freedom of choice for human companionship, so while learning about our dogs, we also need to allow them the time to discover us and to want to be with us. Whatever our expectations are, the dog we choose may not be able to live up to them and give us our dreams – but it will always be able to give us love, and that's far more important.

CHAPTER 5

Understanding the Instincts

I never tire of working with a collie's instincts, and I never grow weary of the time it may take to understand each individual dog. I love the way their characters and their inherited strengths and vulnerabilities tell me about them, and I am inspired when watching dogs in the rescue slowly begin to tell their own story as their natural instincts begin to surface.

If you observe young collies playing, they will play to their strengths, and within those strengths there will be one that loves to stalk, one that is always on the move, one that sits back and observes, and one that takes the lead. If you study them for long enough you will notice that in a large litter, or pack, there will be more than one pup displaying the same strength, while in a smaller litter each one may need to develop a less predominant strength in addition to their stronger one. Usually they are weaned before this team development has really begun, and you would need to be able to study them over a period of time after they are weaned and are looking after themselves.

In fact it's almost impossible to be able to do this, as it's rare that a number of dogs all grow together in the same home, and if they do there will be the human element that will hamper their natural development. But it's important for us to know how they would develop their instincts, and for what purpose. It's also worth noting that a dog taken from such an environment will have developed its strengths to the point where it becomes lost when on its own.

Reading the feature box 'Pack Mentality', we may struggle to imagine how those dogs survived as well as they did, but the most powerful information we can take from them is that they had a strong and fair leader, or parent figure. The other dogs were of two age groups, so there was no other older dog to take over the lead role

Pack Mentality

Due to a family tragedy a group of ten dogs – nine under the age of one, and one two-year-old – were kept in a large building. They were fed once a day, and although the food was meagre, it was enough to sustain them. They grew together as a pack, a family, developing their own roles within that unit; when they came into rescue and were carefully observed, we could soon detect the roles. The pack leader, or the main parent, was the two-year-old, who was clearly in charge. He controlled the dogs and their food, he ate and he made sure the strong ones ate, but his role as leader also meant that the very young ones had enough left-over food to be able to survive and continue to develop.

So they honed in on their pack instincts, the strong, calm one taking control – thus the fit ones, who would have been the hunters, received a reasonable ration of the food, while the younger ones had less food, as they were not able to hunt and therefore their energy requirements were less. They were a family, a pack, and their instincts came to the fore. But because they were penned up in a building they couldn't actually hunt and run free.

All the dogs were rehabilitated and successfully rehomed, although the leader struggled for a long time at having to be part of a unit instead of leading it.

had the two-year-old not been there. Imagine ten very young children all of the same age without a parent or an older sibling.

Instinct can be a very powerful force therefore it is better that we work with it and manage it, rather than ignore it or try to change it. This isn't difficult when training collies for sheep work; if they have a very strong eye they are given less training where they would use the power of the eye, and more on keeping moving. If a dog is a natural driving dog then it doesn't need to work on that skill, therefore it is given other things to learn. In other words, just as in the groups of dogs in paragraph two, a dog's instincts need recognizing and then making sure that the predominant one is not over played – thus allowing other ones to develop. Unless you have a reason for encouraging the strongest instinct, for example, a shepherd with several dogs will work them as a team so the instincts will balance within the team, but a shepherd with one dog will encourage that dog to use all its instincts to the best of its ability. In your home you need your dog to be balanced, so once you have recognized the strongest instinct you can manage it so that it doesn't take over.

A Strong Eye Instinct

A collie with a strong eye is going to stare at everything, and to begin with, it may cause amusement. He will stare at the television, at the cat, at the traffic, in fact anything that catches his eye will cause him to lie down, or go into a stalk position, and stare. But we need to remember that this is his basic instinct, and to him he is holding the movement in his gaze so that it can be caught. In the shepherding world he is keeping a sheep 'hypnotized' with his stare so the shepherd can catch the sheep. But if nobody catches the object of his focus then he is in a frozen state until it moves, then it's down to him to stop it escaping.

Depending on the strength of his eye power he may just stare and then stalk any movement, but because his working instinct isn't coming to fruition he will begin to make his own decision. He may try to 'nip' the object of his stare to make it behave, or if it moves quickly, for example a cat, a bicycle, a car, then he may feel the need to give chase. He can't help his instinct: it is what makes him a good collie. If it is allowed, or even encouraged to develop rather than balancing it with his other instincts, we can see how it can confuse and even upset him.

When a dog is stalking it becomes so focused that it will switch off from surrounding sound, including your voice. The dog that stalks from a standing or semi-crouched position is more likely to 'tune in' to you.

The dog that stalks from a crouched position is so focused it will rarely hear you. Without training this dog could chase if it can't control the movement by herding it. The lower the stalk position, the more focused the dog, making eye power its strongest instinct.

A man who looks into a collie's eye to receive an icy stare is but a fool.
Be at one with man's best friend and through his eyes you will see his very soul.

The Amber Eye

If we take a quick look back to Chapter 3, to the box 'Fight or Flight', we see that the distance where a dog can take control or turn away is like our personal space. When someone approaches the amber-eyed dog and reaches the perimetre of that space, the dog will seek to take control. The degree of control and the area of space will be dictated

The dog has seen someone approaching.

His guardian has not taken over, so he has turned back to face the threat. He has tried to turn away but that failed, so now he must make a decision. If the person continues to approach he may lower his head and growl, and if that fails he may leap forwards.

The person has now entered the dog's space, and the dog is showing he is unhappy.

not just by the eye, but also by the other inherited genes. Let us look at a possible scenario of an amber-eyed dog – regardless of other genetic influences – walking on a lead with his guardian when someone approaches. If that person ignores the dog and walks past, allowing a reasonable amount of space, the dog will more than likely take little notice of them. If the person's approach is more towards the dog, then they will be encroaching on the edge of the dog's personal space. The dog may try to make eye contact, almost inviting the person to stare back, and if the person approaching does look at the dog then the scene is set.

The two people involved may be blissfully unaware of what is going on in the dog's mind at this point, and the person approaching may even smile at the dog, but the dog is now feeling threatened. In his mind it is his job to control the situation, to keep the object of his focus on the edge of his space, and if he can do that, either one of them is free to turn and walk away. But unaware of the dog's thought process, the person thinks the dog is wanting to make contact, so takes a step forwards – and the dog now

---

A Dog's Personal Space

We should respect the personal space of dogs of all breeds. Most people will react adversely if a total stranger stands directly in front of them. A stranger approaching a child with the offer of physical contact, or a treat, is not acceptable under any circumstances. Yet we often fail to give that same respect and protection to dogs. A simple movement of placing your body in front of your dog, as you would with a child, offers protection and safety, and also initiates a strong bond of trust between guardian and dog.

---

has someone in his space.

Turning away is now not an option, so he issues a warning growl, which will often set off a chain of events. The person in the dog's space will be alarmed and the guardian will be mortified. A strong person in the dog's space may give the dog a feeling he is being dominated, while a nervous person will make the dog feel dominant. The dog will automatically be pulled back, but this will make him want to resist and pull forwards, and at least one of the two people concerned may feel panic.

Whatever the outcome, we now have someone who may be apprehensive or even nervous of dogs, a guardian who is scared for what his dog may do next, and a dog who has discovered that if he takes control of a situation, it is resolved. But he is a dog, and doesn't understand that how he resolved it can cause a lot more problems, or even cost him his home or his life.

The above scenario is hypothetical, but I have been presented with many similar cases on consultations, and the dog is nearly always in front of his guardian. If not in front he believes he has to control a situation that his guardian, to his mind, isn't controlling. We know the dog's instinct is to 'hold' the sheep in his gaze until the shepherd can catch the sheep. If the shepherd doesn't give him permission to single out a sheep, then the well-trained dog will stand back. The collie knows the difference between human and sheep, but his instinct will come to the fore when he is presented with a situation that, in

his mind, has to be controlled. Even just his head in front of his guardian's leg means he is taking the lead, so the solution is for the guardian to take control by standing in front of the dog. The handler is now refusing permission for the dog to take control. Once standing behind someone, the personal space takes on a new dimension, as the approach distance from dog to stranger is now blocked, and the guardian is taking up the position of protector and the one who makes the decisions.

Eye Colour and Inherited Traits

Now we can look at eye colour with the different instincts and genes. A short-coated, tri-coloured collie with pricked-up ears and an amber eye is likely to be super sensitive and will react immediately to a person, or another dog, entering his space. This dog may begin with fear, but can become dominant in order to protect himself. The same amber eye in a black-and-white, longer-coated dog with less pricked-up ears will react in the same way, but if this dog feels the need to defend itself it will not be because it is dominant, it will be from fear, and not from a wish to take over.

The hazel-eyed dog is capable of 'holding' a sheep with its gaze, but will not become fixed into the stare like the amber-eyed dog. This dog is not as protective of its space, or as reactive as the amber-eyed one, but if it is a short-coated dog with pricked-up ears we need to remember that even if it accepts someone in its space, it is very sensitive and may feel uncertain if the person is a stranger.

Note

The lighter the eye, the more a dog will feel the need to control movement; the darker the eye, the less it feels the need to control.

If a collie has a really strong instinct we need to work less with that so that his other instincts can come into balance. A collie with a strong eye will try and control

Collies are very patient dogs, and it is a side of their nature that needs encouraging; even a dog with a strong eye can sit and observe patiently without trying to take control.

any movement it sees, and in a home there is plenty of variety: the television, bicycles, lawn mower, hosepipe and balls, just to mention a few, and to begin with it may cause amusement, especially with a puppy. But by allowing it to happen, we are in fact encouraging the one thing that can cause problems as the puppy matures. This pup needs to learn a 'leave' command, and to wait before going for a ball or any form of movement. It would also benefit from calm mind games.

A Gathering Instinct

A collie with a gathering instinct will run out wide around his flock. He will have a good eye, but it won't be so strong that he just wants to focus on one sheep. He will happily sweep round the back of a flock and keep them all together in a tidy group. Collies like to control movement, so away from sheep and with nothing to control he will settle down, but if introduced to a group he may feel the need to control it. He doesn't see a family, a group of children or other dogs as sheep, he's far too clever to make that mistake, but he will see them as an unruly gathering, or a divided group that needs immediate attention. He has no desire to hurt anyone – rather, his intention is to get together a solid group that is safe from harm or from straying. Excitement or noise from children or

A collie is trained to use his skills to keep sheep together, either on a trials course or with a large flock, so imagine his frustration when a group of people separate and he hasn't been taught that this is acceptable and that he doesn't need to control it.

other dogs can actually prevent him from thinking about his task in a calm manner, and this can cause him to become so determined to take control that he nudges or even gives a little nip. He is not being aggressive, he is simply following an instinct that hasn't previously been balanced, and he is frustrated.

If this is his strong instinct he needs to learn that it isn't his responsibility: going round and checking on the group is fine, but if he begins to get stressed, running from one person to another or trying to take control, it is better to put him on a lead and encourage him to calm down. While he doesn't have the same obsession that a strong-eyed dog might have, he is still following a basic instinct that can get him into trouble if he starts using his gathering skills on a group of dogs. If his instinct isn't too strong he may get away with it, but with a strong instinct he will begin to try and control the other dogs, which can be upsetting for both dogs and humans.

A Driving Instinct

A collie with a driving instinct is not unlike the dog with a powerful eye, but he is happy to keep moving. His eye will be powerful enough for him to be able to take control, but whereas the really strong-eyed dog can be almost confrontational, the driving dog will want his sheep to move. In the home he will stalk the cat, the lawnmower and the wheelbarrow. As long as they keep moving, so will he, but if they stop he will not be happy to stand and stare like the strong-eyed dog, and if they run he will run after them in an endeavour to maintain control. This dog's natural instinct is not to run round and prevent the escape, it is to push the object of his focus into an area such as a corner or a wall, where he can keep control.

This collie needs to learn to 'leave' when told, and should be encouraged to move on to something new immediately. If his instinct is not managed while he is on a walk, for example, he will begin to look for something to stalk. If he sees dogs playing, unlike the gathering dog, this collie will 'power walk' towards them, and not understanding their interaction with each other, he will try and stop them by breaking up the group. He will then become frustrated as they are no longer together, and because he isn't working sheep and doesn't have the help of a team player, he will feel lost, and will either freeze on the spot or take to nipping the other dogs.

When we take a collie into our homes, we are not just

Digby was used to seeing the lawnmower in the garden – he even used it as a step to spy through a window. In stages we got him used to seeing it move silently (pushing it), then to hearing the motor and to being told to 'leave it'. He was never allowed in the garden when it was mowing, but neither was he ever afraid of it or wanted to chase it. You can do this with any machinery, including the vacuum cleaner.

taking in a dog, we are taking in years of history and strong instincts, coupled with intelligence and sensitivity. It's a huge responsibility, but it's also a journey of discovery and fun. The fun part for me is, without a doubt, figuring out just who I have inside the lovely collie dog I'm presented with. What is its strongest instinct? How sensitive is it, how much natural energy does it have? And is it going to accept my direction, or is it going to question me? We should never see working with a collie as a struggle or a challenge: we need to understand its thoughts and work with it. Collies are incredibly clever, and their natural instincts are to work *with* someone, be it another dog or a person, and all we need to do is to understand them and tap into that instinct.

Summary

A collie's eyes are powerful and are an amazing guide as to how strong its instincts are.

They are also storytellers, as the eyes will relate to us feelings of pain, confidence, happiness and fear, and coupled with what we have learned about dogs' instincts and colour genes, we can begin to really see each one differently. This is not just because they are all individual, but because their different characters indicate how we need to manage them in different ways. If we understand the instincts and how to balance them, it will make any problem solving much easier.

The instinct to control movement should be in every collie but it should never be a problem. They have the power in their stance and their eye to challenge a defiant sheep, but they can be gentle with lambs, even when they are running. They just need to learn what they can control and what they should leave alone.

CHAPTER 6

Choosing your Dog

Which do you think is going to be the right choice for you? Could it be a puppy, a young dog, an older dog, or a rescue dog? Rather than deciding what you want, it could be best to work out which would be right for you, your commitments, your way of life, and your experience. Hopefully you have not come straight to this section, as the previous chapters provide information on the diversity of the breed, and are also a guide as to what may be a good choice for you. For example, if you have never had a collie before, then a short-coated, prick-eared, amber-eyed dog may not be the best choice for you. At this point someone may be thinking: but I have already made that choice, so now what do I do? This chapter is about choosing the collie to have in your life, and is not about the one you already have, which we will cover later.

Dreams of a lovely cuddly puppy may need to be put on hold if you have a busy life and won't be able to commit to the time and dedication that a puppy needs. So could a young dog be a better choice? But there is usually a reason why a young dog is in need of rehoming, and it is often because it has developed some issues: so are you experienced enough to be able to work with those issues? The older dog may simply be a lovely dog whose previous guardian can no longer keep it due to ill health or family circumstances; and the rescue dog might come from a similar background as the old dog, or it could have issues not unlike the young one in need of a home.

Taking a dog into your home is a huge responsibility, and all of the above apply to any breed of dog. Whatever you choose, it will be yours from the minute you take it, puppy or adult, into your home. Therefore it's important that before you make that decision you know as much as possible about the dog you are thinking of taking into your life, and about the person or organization you are getting it from.

Puppies are lovely and cuddly, but they do need a lot of time and commitment; the one that comes to the front may be choosing you, but he may also be the nosey one of the litter.

59

Choosing a Puppy

Puppies are irresistible. They are lovely and cuddly and so dependent, but if finding the right litter to choose from is difficult, then selecting a puppy from that litter is even harder. For that reason you need to make sure you know what you are looking for, and what would be right for you. Whoever the breeder of the litter is, you need to go armed with questions. How many breeding bitches do they have, and how many litters a year do they produce? Can you see both parents, and if not, can you have information about the sire and where he can be seen? Are there any dogs from previous litters available for you to see? The answer to those questions will tell you a lot about the breeder and the pups. If they are registered with the International Sheep Dog Society (ISDS) or the Kennel Club (KC) it will give some idea of their breeding, but it is no guarantee that they are compatible. You may find it difficult to get any of the relevant information about puppies you find for sale in local papers or on advertising websites.

Once the decision has been made to have a puppy, it's natural to want it as soon as possible, but it is worth taking the time to look around and to think very carefully, not just about the puppy but also about the person who

has bred it. Are they breeding commercially or purely for the money, and do the dogs and puppies appear to be well looked after? On a personal note if I were looking for a puppy I would want one from someone who is breeding because they want to keep one for themselves, as that would help me to believe they had chosen the breeding line with care. It would be even better if they had their own line of dogs, as there would be some of the same breeding that I could see. I would also look for a puppy from a working line, regardless of whether its parents were working or whether I wanted it to work.

I love the breed, so would want a puppy with all the qualities that make the breed so special – but I would also make sure that it would be different to the puppy I might have chosen in my youth. Then I would have been happy to take on a pup that I knew would challenge me, but now, since advancing years have made me more cautious, I would go for a pup with a calming influence in its gene pool.

Who Chooses Who

I have no doubt that there are times when a puppy knows who it wants to be with, and you look at the pup and every fibre of your being tells you that this pup is the right one for

I would always choose the puppy who stayed at the back, the one who seemed to be deciding whether I was worth his attention. But the type of puppy who is right for one person won't necessarily be right for another.

you. But sometimes the pup that appears to choose someone is simply the boldest of the litter and the nosiest, but by coming forwards you notice it, and it seems to be the right one for you. But when he leaves the litter another one will step forward in his place, and that puppy will appear to choose the next person who looks at them.

Personally I have never chosen the pup that came to the front. I know a lot of people would say that the bold one in the litter will be a confident pup, and the one at the back will be nervous, but it's the one at the back weighing me up that has always been the one to catch my eye: sensitive and inquisitive but not nosey, and bright enough to want to get to know me first.

At this point we need to understand that the bold one can become a nervous wreck, and the one that hangs back can become a bully, because although breeding and genetics play a huge part, a lack of understanding of the breed can spoil a well bred dog, whereas an understanding of the breed can turn a dubiously bred pup into an amazing dog.

Choosing a Rescue Dog

Taking any dog into your life is a huge commitment, whether it is a puppy or a rescue dog, but if a puppy develops issues you should be able to trace back to when and how they began. With a rescue dog, you won't have that information. Try to stay away from rescues that allow you to walk round and look at all the dogs, because at some point you may be in danger of letting your heart rule your head. I've had far too many people come to me with a problem dog because they just couldn't bear to leave it in the rescue centre, but as a result they were out of their depth and the dog's problems were increasing instead of decreasing.

If you are choosing a rescue dog, make sure you get as much information as possible from the rescue centre, and make sure you will be able to manage any issues there might be.

If the rescue centre is willing to let you take your chosen dog home the same day, don't be afraid to tell them you need time to think about it. You need to be absolutely certain that not only is it the right dog for you, but that you can work with any issues it may have. Ask the rescue if they have any background information about the dog: if it has come from a private home they will have some, but if it is a stray then they won't know anything about its past. Ask how long they have had it in their rescue, and if it's only a few days, don't be afraid to question how well they have assessed it. Assessing a dog takes weeks, and the longer they have had it in their care, the more they should know about it.

Find out if the dog you are looking at has already been rehomed recently by the centre and has been brought back to them, and ask why, and what the issues were. It is worth asking the questions and finding out as much as you can to avoid the sadness to both yourself and the dog if you find you can't manage some issues that you had not previously known about.

If you have had a rescue dog before, you will be familiar with some of the usual settling-in problems – but as we learned in the first chapters, collies are not all the same, and issues in some can be harder to deal with than in others. The high energy dogs in a rescue, such as the short-coated ones or the ones with light eyes, are more likely to have issues that will require experience and a lot of patience. Even if you have had experience with such dogs, ask the rescue what their policy is after rehoming. Do they offer back-up, and do they employ people with the experience to help you if there are issues?

An Older Dog

Not everyone is prepared to take on an older dog, but they have so much to offer and they deserve to have someone to love them. Granted it depends on their past, and again, whether a dog is from a rescue or a private home, the questions about its background still need to be asked. The most common reasons for an older dog needing a home is either due to a family bereavement or illness. I won't say they all come with no issues, but serious issues are rare – it's usually a matter of mild arthritis or a heart murmur, neither of which will cause major problems. Retired farm dogs are usually really quiet, easy dogs as they have worked all their lives, and when suddenly given an 'all mod cons' retirement home they soon settle in.

Not everyone is prepared to take home an older dog, but they can be such a joy and we can learn a lot from them.

Making Himself at Home

Many years ago a friend of mine lived near to a hill shepherd. She would watch him working his sheep, and would tell him that when he retired his old dog he should give him to her. When the old dog began to tire of his work the shepherd took her at her word and retired his dog with her. She spent a whole day organizing her integral garage into a pen for him so he would feel at home. Bless him: he walked into her kitchen, lay down by her Aga, and never once set foot in the 'pen' she had made for him.

Sometimes older dogs can be great teachers, especially for someone who has never had a dog before. Being an older dog doesn't mean they are not capable of going for long walks, enjoying holidays, and sharing fun times with you. Although their time with you may be short, it will be full of fun and learning.

A Younger Dog

You may decide that the best choice for you is a young dog, one that is out of the puppy and house-training stage, and although not an old dog, one that is mature enough not to pose too many problems. Remember that from six months to about two years old they are adolescents, and sometimes the problems that have been overcome as a puppy have been replaced with other issues. One young

By taking on a young dog you should be avoiding the house training and the initial puppy training, but they are adolescents for a long time, and although no longer puppies, they still require the same time and commitment.

dog may be lacking in confidence and feel insecure, but another can be over-confident and dominant with other dogs. The advantage of being young means they are not likely to be too set in their ways, but you may need to be prepared to put in some hard work.

A Dog From a Private Home

Newspapers and websites are often full of advertisements for dogs that are 'for sale' or 'free to a good home'. You need to be really careful if you go down this avenue, as you cannot guarantee that any information provided is genuine. If the dog is from someone you know and can trust, you should have no problems – but always make sure that you check who the dog is microchipped to, and ask to see the certificate to make sure it is chipped to the person you are getting it from. Once you buy or take a dog from such an advert it is rare that you would have any comeback if the dog turns out to be very aggressive or has issues beyond anything you can manage.

Being Positive

Taking any dog into your life is a huge responsibility, requiring patience, understanding and dedication, plus a lot of research into the right time and the right dog

Speed, stamina and intelligence: collies can change direction in the wink of an eye, keep their balance and not once lose sight of the sheep that is breaking away – and at the same time they will be working out how to solve the problem.

Your view: your eyes will be drawn to the bridge and beyond it. There is plenty to see: someone walking in the distance who may have a dog with them, houses and fields.

Your dog's view: his eyes will not see any of the things that you can see. He sees the stream, and under the bridge is an escape route. You may think the area is secure, but a collie who likes to investigate has seen a path to freedom that you never thought of.

for you. Once you take a collie into your home you must appreciate that they are an energetic, fun-loving breed. They are also born to work and to be part of a team, so in your plans for having one you need to make sure that you can provide the time for both you and your dog to be creative together. This doesn't just mean making sure they have plenty of physical exercise in the hope that this will tire them out for the rest of the day. On the contrary, they may take a short rest but the more they run, the more stamina they will have, and the more they will want to run. It doesn't mean a lot of exercise is bad for them, but it isn't necessary: they need a sensible amount of physical exercise, but they also need to work mentally.

If you go out for a run and come back tired you will soon be ready for more exercise, but if you go out for a run and solve a problem at the same time, you will be mentally tired as well as physically – and this is what a collie needs. When they are working sheep they are running over rough ground and keeping their balance, while at the same time working out which sheep may cause a problem and how best to deal with it. This is what they are good at: they love problems, and the problems don't have to be complicated, but they do need to be a challenge, and the dog needs to be kept calm while trying to work it out.

An older dog may be happy to spend less time doing either physical or mental exercise, but unless their health dictates otherwise, they still need both brain and body to be kept as active as possible.

The time to have any doubts is when you are looking for the right dog, but once you have decided which type of collie to go for, what age, where from, and whether you are ready for the commitment, it's time to be positive. Collies are very sensitive, and if you are lacking in confidence your dog will soon sense it, and although you don't want your new dog or puppy to be over-confident and trying to take over your home, neither do you want it to feel insecure or vulnerable. The requirements of a puppy and how to settle it into a new home will be different for an older dog or one from a rescue, but there are two things they need above anything else: they need their own space – somewhere where they can feel safe and where they can go in times of uncertainty – and they need time.

Through the Dog's Eyes

One of the best things we can do for our dogs is to see the world from their perspective, but be prepared for a surprise when you discover how complicated we are, and how straightforward and effortless the dog needs its life to be. Throughout the rest of the book we will see how teaching something new or solving a problem need not be difficult if we first look at what the dog is thinking. For example, a dog often pulls on a lead because it believes it is the right thing to do, simply because its guardian has encouraged it – but when we stop and look at how the dog has perceived the lead-walking lessons, it becomes clear what we need to do.

More about lead walking later; for now we need to look at the dog entering a new home. Have you made sure you have at least two different beds for your dog, some toys, a ball, a ball thrower and, of course, some treats? Have you booked a vet's appointment for the first week to make sure the vet and your dog get on well? Have you planned all the walks you are going to go in the first week, and have you booked in at a training class or puppy training? I hope you have not done even the half of these things, because the last thing your new dog or puppy needs is to be so overwhelmed that it can't cope.

You only need the vet in the first week if your dog is poorly. You have wanted this dog for a long time, but to your dog you are a stranger, and suddenly you take it to another stranger who is going to be quite personal with it in the course of a vet check. How would you react to that if you were the dog? Another situation is that your dog may be so used to toys that it bounds in, sees how many you have provided, and thinks it has moved into toy heaven, and that you don't count. Or it may never have seen toys before, and may not even want them.

Your dog or puppy has just been taken from what was familiar – and even a rescue kennel is familiar – by someone who is still a stranger, and moved into a house it has never seen before. With a whole new set of sights and smells to learn about, it needs a lot of time to adjust and to work out its new life. Your most precious gift to your new dog is time and patience.

Summary

When you take a new dog or puppy into your life it is going to be for the rest of that dog's life, so it is worth taking that extra time and care to choose the right dog and the right age group for you. Keep in mind the type of collie that would be best suited to you and your life-style, or to your family. Don't be tempted to get the first dog or pup you see without finding out as much as possible about its background, and make sure you are given time to go away and think about it. Nobody should be happy to let you, a stranger, walk off with their dog. They should want to know about you, and they should want some thinking time as well. When you have chosen your dog you are committing to giving it a life of love and security; and your next great gifts are time and patience.

Who could refuse the appealing 'take me home please' look that a collie can give? But make sure you are choosing a dog that you can understand and that will be right for you and your way of life.

CHAPTER 7

The Next Step: Preparing for your Dog's Arrival

We have gone through the history of the breed, its instincts, its life on the farm, the different characters, and choosing your dog, so it would seem logical that the next step is taking your dog home. But there is one huge step forwards that I would ask you to take before you make that final commitment. The last thing I want to do is make you think that having a Border Collie is complicated, so in this chapter I want to try and take away anything that is not necessary, not needed and not always the best option. Instead I want to focus on all the amazing things about a companion collie, and how to keep the intelligence and sensitivity they have whilst retaining all that is calm and peaceful.

Of course you want to give your dog the best, and why wouldn't you? But sometimes the 'best' isn't always the 'right' thing to do. The history of the breed conveys they need little in the way of possessions but a lot in the way of companionship, so let's take it back to basics: your dog needs a comfortable bed, a food bowl, a water bowl, a collar, a lead, a long line and some food. These are essentials, and anything else is an extra. So, before you get your puppy or older dog, think twice about going on a shopping spree and buying a lot of toys: squeaky ones, fluffy ones, balls that light up when they roll, soft balls, a ball thrower, a football, and you can even register them in a training class. Your dog is going to come into your home and think it's Christmas! It's not wrong to want to get these things, and it's fun choosing them, but you don't really know your dog yet, so you can't know what he really

Collies are very uncomplicated, and their ability to amuse themselves needs to be encouraged. This dog amuses himself by throwing a ball into the bush and then diving in to get it back. Not good for the gardener, but great fun for him!

needs or wants. You don't know his likes and dislikes, and believe me it's a lot of fun finding these things out together.

If you buy a child a toy and then spend ages demonstrating how it works, and even longer playing with it, then whose toy is it? It's good for children to be able to

Collies are great mimics, and once you have a close relationship with one it will try and smile back at you.

have their own input, as not only do they learn, but they can also keep themselves amused. You will find plenty of information available telling you that collies love chasing balls, that they have to be kept mentally stimulated, they need to walk for miles every day, they love to round people up and they are often nippy with children. Sadly you will find it far more difficult to find information explaining how they love to chill out, how calm they can be, and how they don't need to have all that exercise or constant mental stimulation.

Everything in the first chapters of this book depicts them as anything but a hyper, ball-obsessed, nippy dog

– so which would you rather have: the intelligent, calm, playful dog, or one that is constantly demanding your attention and doesn't know how to relax?

By taking photographs of a dog in action, or videos and running them back in slow motion, you soon see how a lot of the time its entire weight is on one leg. If it is turning sharply without thinking about what it is doing it can damage its joints or develop arthritis.

If a dog becomes obsessive with a ball, the exercise it is getting usually tires it out – but it can also become footsore.

Obsessive Behaviour

Sadly obsessive behaviour is a phrase often used to describe collies, and to a degree it is true, but as they are not obsessive as puppies, what happens to them to make them so? I tend to see them more as mimics who love to please: for example, if you constantly smile at a dog, a percentage of them will try and smile back. If you say 'hello' to your dog each morning, a percentage will make a sound just like 'hello'. If you jump up and down when excited most dogs will be happy to jump up and down with you. None of *those* behaviours will become obsessive, however the action that gives them the chance to try and control movement *can* become obsessive, especially if it appears to please you.

Calming an Obsession

If I am training a dog to work sheep I have to be careful that it doesn't become the only thing the dog is interested in, because it will become obsessed in its job. I want my dog to work, but also to be my companion: after all, that is in the dog's nature, but it's up to me to balance it. If my dog only wants to go to the sheep field and won't go for exercise unless sheep are involved, then I need to rethink our relationship. I will make sure the dog has days off with no sheep involved, and we will go for walks and work more on our relationship. We will already have a 'leave' command in place, so we will walk around the sheep field with my dog on a lead and will use the 'leave' each time he stops to look at the sheep. I don't want him to think he can't work sheep, so looking and walking is fine. This mixture puts everything back into place, and my dog has learned that being my pal is good 'time out', and the sheep are his work.

There will be plenty of information available from all different sources, but the best advice is to know your own collie. One of these two black-and-white collies could become ball obsessed, and one won't be interested in a ball at all. Do you know which is which?

Remember the ears and the body shape can dilute the light eyes, or they can support the light-eyed gene.

There's nothing wrong with a dog having a ball, but if that ball is in use every day and each walk includes a ball, then it will become an obsession. Before you dismiss me as anti-ball and anti-fun, you have to remember that I see the results when a dog won't recall unless the owner has a ball. It doesn't know what to do on a walk if it isn't chasing after a ball, and dogs that do are worn out and hip sore from chasing a ball for half an hour and more. I also have people who tell me it's so sad that their dog doesn't play with a ball or isn't interested in toys or treats – which I am told makes it so hard to train him! And there I am thinking their dog is happy in his own way, and if you leave him alone he will find his own amusement – but when I explain that possibility, I am informed they don't want him to play on his own, they want to be involved. Then please get down on the floor, talk to him and massage him!

I am not a killjoy, but having a dog is about what the dog needs, and not what we think it has to have, and I do wonder sometimes if we are often the ones who become a little obsessed. Remember Max in Chapter 2: I knew he could be a top class trials dog and I tried so hard to get him to do what I wanted, until it was pointed out to me by a shepherd to listen to my dog and find out what he wanted. We all make mistakes, but the important thing is to learn from them; up to that point I was sure that I always did what was best for my dogs, but being human I had that selfish streak that said I could have a world beater. Max brought me down to earth, and I am so grateful to him for that.

Try not to overload your dog with too much information and too many distractions; the last thing you want is an abundance of toys, balls and outside influences. You need to find out as much about your new family member as possible. Too much information and too many possessions could interfere with your relationship to the point that you are no longer important to your dog unless you have a toy and are playing. You have the rest of your dog's life to introduce all the many things that you would like him to have, so spend the first few weeks getting to know each other and working out what is best for him.

Thoughts on Training

If you have never had a dog or puppy before, you will probably need some help, but don't go and enrol at a training club without first finding out what you need. Not all dogs respond well to classes, and taking an unruly dog to a class can be disruptive for the class and upsetting for both you and your dog. At least one private session could be more beneficial to you both before attending a class, and always ask if you can sit in on a class before joining. If the instructor isn't happy about that, then join and just sit in for a while on the first one. A good trainer will not expect you to ask your dog to do something that clearly upsets it, so never be afraid to voice any concerns you may have.

I am urging you to be cautious and to take your time, not because having a new dog is difficult or because I want to stop you having fun with your dog – on the contrary, I want you to have a well mannered dog that you can take anywhere and do all sorts of fun things with – but it doesn't happen overnight. It is said that prevention is better than cure, and it's true, a high percentage of the collies I see coming in to our rescue are over six months and under two years old, and their owners have given them everything. But giving them everything can turn them into dogs that expect to have whatever they want and on their terms, which is why they end up in rescue needing rehabilitation.

Work at being the one whom everyone envies because your dog is so well mannered and appears so 'easy'; you will know how much work you put into getting this enviable relationship with your dog, but it's far better than being the one whom everybody avoids because your dog is so wayward.

There is no shortage of information to be found both in books and on the internet, and if you ask someone for advice because you need help, suddenly nearly everyone is an expert. Stay calm, keep it simple, and make up your own mind as to what you believe is the best for you and

your dog. Don't keep trying different methods because it will confuse you both, and if things don't seem to be working, sit down with a quiet cup of tea and take some time to figure out where and when it started going wrong. We all make mistakes, but remember to keep reminding yourself: parent first and best friend second. Then your dog will both love and respect you.

Your dog needs a guiding figure, and you can call yourself whatever you choose – pack leader, parent figure, head of the clan, and no doubt there are many more possible terms, but they all mean the same thing: the one in charge, the one who guides and protects, and ultimately the one to whom those under that leadership will turn in times of trouble. From the relationship of mentor and protector you will find the best friendship imaginable.

Your Dog's Own Space

Before we talk about taking your dog or puppy home we need to think about what he needs in terms of his own space. Whether it is a puppy, a rescue dog, or an older dog, nothing in your home is familiar to him. Imagine fostering a small child and bringing them home for the first time: they don't know where the bathroom is, they don't know which rooms they can go in and which they can't, they don't know when mealtimes are. In fact, everything will seem very strange – but give them their own bedroom, where they can feel safe and where they are not under any pressure: then they can settle in and come round in their own time.

Please don't discount using a crate, but let's take away the words 'crate' or 'cage', as neither sounds friendly, and by definition they almost imply that the dog is being imprisoned. Instead substitute the word 'den', and suddenly it takes on a new meaning: it's made to be inviting, with a nice cosy bed, a small treat to nibble and a blanket over it. Why wouldn't a dog love that cosy den where it can be itself, chill out and be safe?

Try to imagine sharing a house with someone you don't know very well. Until you get to know each other you will really value your own room and some privacy, and it will take time to learn about each other's likes and dislikes. Even with someone you know quite well, the first time of living together will probably bring up things you never knew about each other. Imagine the same scenario, but with someone who had no idea they were going to be sharing with you, and neither of you speak the same

Try to think of a crate as your dog's den. A nice bed and a blanket over the top and it is transformed into a cosy retreat. This one even has little sheep on the blanket.

language: how scary is that thought, and how long before you really get to know each other? Now you are seeing your home through your dog's eyes, and understanding what it must be like for him in the first few days.

By providing a secure and safe place you are welcoming your dog without being intrusive, you are letting him know that he is safe, but you are also not putting any pressure on him to get to know you faster than he can manage. Border Collies love to be in small places, they like to have their backs protected when they curl up, and they like to be able see what is going on without being seen. On a farm they will sit proudly on the quad bike and they will love being in the tractor cab, but when it comes to their time to chill out and rest, they will tunnel under

bales of hay, go under an old tractor, or find a quiet corner where they won't be disturbed.

Your home is not a farm, but your dog is a sheepdog by breed and by nature, and sheepdogs like to take stock of things, they like to work out situations, and to do that they need time and space. I have met people who wouldn't use a crate for a den, but cordon off the space under the stairs because that's where the dog liked to be – I think the dog was trying to tell them something! Others give their dog its own room, but that isn't small and cosy and safe like a den, neither can the space under the stairs or a room or anything else that is static be folded up and taken with you. Your dog can have his den in the car, on holiday, visiting friends – it's almost like a child's comfort blanket.

Summary

By now you know the history that is behind the breed, you understand its work ethics and its sensitivity, and you can't wait to get your new dog home. Be excited, and feel all the love and emotion that is yours to feel, for what I hope is one of the best things to happen in your life. One of my mottos is 'if in doubt, leave it out', and I would urge anyone with a dog that if you are not sure what to do, then if possible don't do anything until you have thought it through, and take your time. In rescue we see at first hand the results of rushing a dog and trying to do too much, too soon, until the dog becomes anxious and frustrated. Take some deep breaths, keep calm, and take time to understand your dog. A dog that appears to be lucky and has everything, has nothing if there is no understanding or companionship. The dog that may evoke pity because it seems to have nothing, in fact has everything it needs if it is understood and has a lifelong companion to love, and who loves him.

The calm collie that you see on the beach trotting along with a ball in his mouth might be just how you would like your collie to be, but it doesn't happen overnight. So keep everything very simple and calm for your new dog's arrival, be patient and allow him time to settle in.

CHAPTER 8

Health and Welfare

Nobody can guarantee that their dog will always enjoy good health, and whether he comes from a private source or a rescue, there is always the 'unknown', the health problem that suddenly appears seemingly from nowhere. If this happens, blaming the breeder, the previous owner or the rescue will not change things, but you can help to prevent some illnesses – and should the worst happen you need to be prepared.

Parents are often heard saying that their major financial outgoings began when their children were born, and although dogs don't need school uniforms, Christmas presents and holidays, they do need vaccinations, worming and regular health checks. If you research Border Collies and health problems you will find a lot of conflicting advice, and some of it can be quite scary. Remember this is a very old and a very strong breed; Border Collies are stoic, and will rarely complain if they are feeling under the weather, so you need to know your dog well enough to be able to detect a change in him – something else that takes time, but can pay dividends as he grows older. The fact that they are stoic may make it hard to detect a problem, but it also means that they will never give up. They really do live for the day, and you will rarely catch a collie feeling genuinely sorry for himself; he may try to gain a bit of sympathy, but show him an open door and it will be business as usual.

I love the breed, and I love delving into their minds and seeing life as they see it, but I am no vet, and if there are any health problems with my dogs then I seek professional advice. For that reason I would not try to give

A collie needs you to help him to keep fit and healthy, and the best start you can give your dog will pay dividends when he gets older.

Collies are stoic, and sometimes it isn't easy to recognize the onset of an illness, but with regular health checks from your vet, your dog should be able to enjoy a lovely peaceful retirement.

advice on something that only a vet can do. I am very lucky in having Peter O'Hagan as a good friend. He is Ambassador for Welfare for the FOSTBC rescue, and a brilliant vet who was happy to go through some of the questions he is regularly asked by owners of collies to give you an insight into any possible health issues and how to deal with them. The remainder of this chapter is kindly contributed by Peter O'Hagan, BVMS Cert AVP (GSAS) MRCVS.

Managing Health Problems

Many diseases in dogs can be prevented with appropriate vaccination, worming, anti-parasite treatment and neu-

tering. Others, such as hip dysplasia and collie eye, can be reduced through careful selection of breeding stock.

Why Vaccines?

Distemper and Adenovirus

Infectious diseases such as distemper and adenovirus (canine infectious hepatitis) have largely been eradicated from the UK through widespread vaccination of the dog population. However, as the number of UK unvaccinated dogs is currently increasing, cases of distemper are once again being reported. Distemper usually starts as a respiratory problem causing a thick green discharge from the eyes and nose, but it can progress to cause other signs such as fever, diarrhoea, thickened pads and seizures. Canine adenovirus is very rare, but typically causes clouding of the eyes and liver failure.

Parvovirus and Leptospirosis

More commonly encountered infectious diseases in the UK are parvovirus and leptospirosis ('lepto' is especially serious as it can pass from dogs to humans, and vice versa).

Parvovirus typically affects younger, unvaccinated dogs and causes severe vomiting and diarrhoea, which can prove fatal. The virus is spread by dogs coming into contact with diarrhoea from infected dogs. Once recovered, dogs will continue to shed the virus for eight weeks, and it is very difficult to eliminate from the environment. The virus can survive up to two years – this is important if you are considering taking on a new dog after losing one to parvovirus.

Leptospirosis can be contracted by dogs coming into contact with infected urine from rats, mice, foxes, cattle, horses, wildlife, humans or other dogs. The disease affects the liver and kidneys and is often severe or fatal.

Dogs can be protected against all these diseases with an appropriate vaccination course. Leptospirosis continues to be challenging, because current UK vaccines only protect against a maximum of four commonly encountered strains, and there are strains in circulation for which there is currently no vaccine available.

Whether a working collie or a companion, a healthy coat, a bright eye and a supple body are a joy to see.

Worming

Worming dogs regularly is essential to reduce the risk of diseases passing to humans (such as Toxocara, which causes blindness in children) and livestock (tapeworm infections can pass from dogs to sheep). It can also prevent lungworm. Pet dogs should be wormed every three months with a broad spectrum wormer such as Milbemax, or monthly in young dogs or those in high-risk areas for lungworm (currently the south of England and Wales). Some collies are inherently sensitive to some of the drugs in wormers, such as Milbemax, but these medicines can generally be used safely if the correct dose for the bodyweight of the dog is carefully calculated.

Farm dogs are at higher risk of passing on tapeworms to sheep so should be wormed every six weeks with a product containing praziquantel, and after dosing should be kept off the land for two days. Where public access to land is permitted it is essential that dog owners pick up any dog faeces as worm larvae can survive on the land for up to three years.

Ticks

Ticks pose a threat to dogs and humans because they carry diseases such as Lyme disease. Ticks in the UK are seasonal, peaking in spring and autumn, and are generally found in long grass or marshy areas. Ticks tend to attach to the head, neck, lower body and legs, so it is wise to check over your dog for ticks after walking in these areas. Regular treatment with anti-tick medication such as Bravecto or Credelio will eliminate the risk of infection. If attempting to remove a tick from your dog it is essential to use a proper tick remover, twisting the entire tick off to avoid leaving the tick mouthparts embedded in the dog's skin.

Emerging Diseases

Several infectious diseases are now classed as 'emerging' in UK dogs – largely due to increased pet travel to Europe, and the importation of dogs from abroad. If you are planning to travel abroad or import a dog it is important to check the local risks of diseases such as Leishmania (in the Mediterranean and southern Europe), which is spread by sandflies, and Babesia, which is spread by ticks.

Alabama Rot

Alabama rot is a term that originated to describe a disease affecting racing Greyhounds in southern USA in the late 1980s. It subsequently emerged in the UK in 2012, and is also known as cutaneous and renal glomerular vasculopathy (CRGV). The cause of the disease is unknown, but typically it affects dogs in the south and west of the UK between November and May. Ulcers typically form on the skin of the face, tongue, lower limbs and lower body. Some dogs go on to develop severe life-threatening kidney injury, whereas some only develop skin lesions and subsequently recover. There appears to be no specific cure, but dogs without severe kidney injury will often respond well to non-specific medical treatment.

Neutering

Apart from helping to prevent unwanted litters of pups, neutering is known to help prevent certain diseases such as testicular and breast cancer, womb infections (pyometra) and prostatic abscesses, and certain types of hernia that affect male dogs. Recently some studies have shown links between early neutering and certain types of joint diseases (hip dysplasia and cruciate ligament disease), and also incontinence in female dogs and the development of certain tumours. None of the studies looked specifically at Border Collies, however from the available evidence it would be wise to delay neutering in Border Collies until they have reached a minimum of one year old.

Other Conditions of Particular Importance to the Border Collie

Hip Dysplasia

This term describes a developmental condition whereby the growing dog's hip joints fail to form an optimal smooth 'ball and socket' joint and instead form with irregularities in various parts of the joints. This leads to arthritis and lameness as the dog matures. Affected dogs can experience wide variations in the impact of the condition on their quality of life, so managing the disease has to be tailored to the individual dog. Various 'conservative' treatments (diet, painkillers, physiotherapy, joint supplements) or more aggressive surgical treatments (including total hip replacements) exist.

Because of the hereditary genetic nature of the disease, dogs intended for breeding can be screened for the disease once they are over one year old. X-rays of the hips are sent to the British Veterinary Association for hip scoring, and results are published by the Kennel Club. Dogs do not have to be KC registered to be hip-scored. A low score is desirable, and for breeding Border Collies this should ideally be less than the breed median (average) score, which is currently ten.

Collie Eye Anomaly (CEA)

This condition is actually more prevalent in other collie breeds (rough, smooth and Sheltie); however, the potential impact on Border Collies is higher because of the requirements for good eyesight when working. CEA is genetic and affects the development of the sensory functions of the eye from birth. It is much easier to detect in pups (six to eight weeks old) because once the eye starts to mature at around twelve weeks, the signs of the disease are much easier to miss on examination. The developmental problems rarely cause blindness in the adult dog unless other secondary problems develop (in up to a third of affected dogs). These secondary issues usually occur within the first few years of life.

Screening pups for CEA can be done through the BVA eye scheme from five to twelve weeks of age. There are also genetic tests available to check for CEA, as well as primary lens luxation (PLL) and progressive retinal atrophy (PRA) – these conditions being rarer. These tests are usually done with a cotton-bud cheek swab. Affected dogs should not be used for breeding.

Epilepsy

Epilepsy in dogs is usually idiopathic (no identified cause), although blood tests and scans can be performed to rule out other potential causes of seizures. Idiopathic epilepsy usually affects dogs under eight years of age; other causes are more likely if a dog older than this starts to show signs of seizures.

Border Collies affected by idiopathic epilepsy tend to experience more severe seizures from a younger age than other breeds. They are also more likely to require treatment with several different types of drug, as opposed to other breeds, which might be more likely to need treatment with just a single drug. The life expectancy of Border Collies diagnosed with epilepsy from a young age therefore tends to be relatively short (an average of just two years in one scientific study), partly because of the intensive treatment required, and partly because of the severity of the seizures they experience.

Epileptic dogs should not be used for breeding as there is a strong pedigree association with epilepsy. It is also important to let your vet know if your dog shows any signs of seizure activity; these can start as just mild muscle twitches, which may not yet have progressed to full seizures.

Drug Sensitivity

Up to 59 per cent of collies have a mutated gene (MDR1 deletion) that makes them more sensitive to the effects of certain drugs: Milbemycin/Moxidectin (commonly found in dog worming tablets), Ivermectin (commonly used for parasite control in cattle, sheep and small pets such as guinea pigs and rabbits), Acepromazine and Butorphanol (sedative drugs), Digoxin (heart medication) and Vincristine (cancer therapy).

These drugs can generally be used safely in collies if there are no suitable alternatives, but close attention must be paid to accurate dosing. Always avoid treating with multiple medication that might each contain the relevant drugs (for example, giving Milbemax worming tablets and Advocate spot-on flea treatment at the same time would be more of a risk because they each contain Milbemycin/Moxidectin). If dogs experience any adverse effects with any of these drugs this information should be passed on to your vet, who will note and report it accordingly.

Vestibular Disease and Border Collies

Vestibular disease (VD) affects older dogs (the average age of onset is twelve years), and often develops acutely. The signs can mimic a stroke, and include tilting of the head, flickering of the eyes, problems with balance, vomiting, or even collapse. The affected areas of the body are the inner ear (peripheral VD) or the brain (central VD), and these can be damaged because of infection, trauma, tumours, age-related degeneration or problems affecting the blood supply. The disease affects many breeds of dog, but Border Collies are one of the most commonly affected – although this is a relatively rare problem affecting only two to three dogs per 1,000.

Because of the wide variety of possible causes, the dog's chances of recovery and its response to treatment can be quite variable. Diagnosis of the problem can be difficult, but most dogs are treated without a definite diagnosis being reached, and often improve with relatively inexpensive medical therapy.

The signs of disease often come on quickly and dramatically, but although the underlying cause may not always be identified, the chances of recovery with prompt veterinary attention are reasonable. In one study 41 per cent of dogs made improvements within four days of the disease onset; only 16 per cent failed to improve. Dogs often do not recover fully, and may continue to have balance issues; however, they may continue to have a good quality of life following recovery.

CHAPTER **9**

Your Puppy

It's an exciting time taking your new dog home for the first time. You have probably been waiting for this day for a long time, and now it's finally arrived – but the first few days, or in some cases the first few hours, can set a pattern for weeks to come. It doesn't mean you can't do all the things you may have planned, but you do need to be careful before launching into something that might make your dog think he doesn't need to have some boundaries. Because they are all different, and each age group will need a different approach, we will start with a puppy.

A New Puppy

Anyone who says they don't make a fuss of a puppy just can't be telling the truth, not if they love dogs. They are just wonderful little beings, and you would have to be really hard to not want to cuddle them. But you need to look at the world through their eyes to be able to see how they feel when you take them home.

Your pup's first few weeks may have been in someone's house, in a professional whelping pen or a farm building, but wherever it was, it would be different from your home. He may have come from a rescue or from a puppy farm, and although your home is the start of the rest of his life, he doesn't know that. As yet he won't be walking on a lead so you will be carrying him into your house, and those big puppy eyes have a lot to take in. So far his life will have been with siblings or other dogs, and suddenly they're not there – and even if your pup has lived alone, he won't know anything different, so humans suddenly fussing over him can be very overwhelming.

Allow your pup time to take things in, and provide

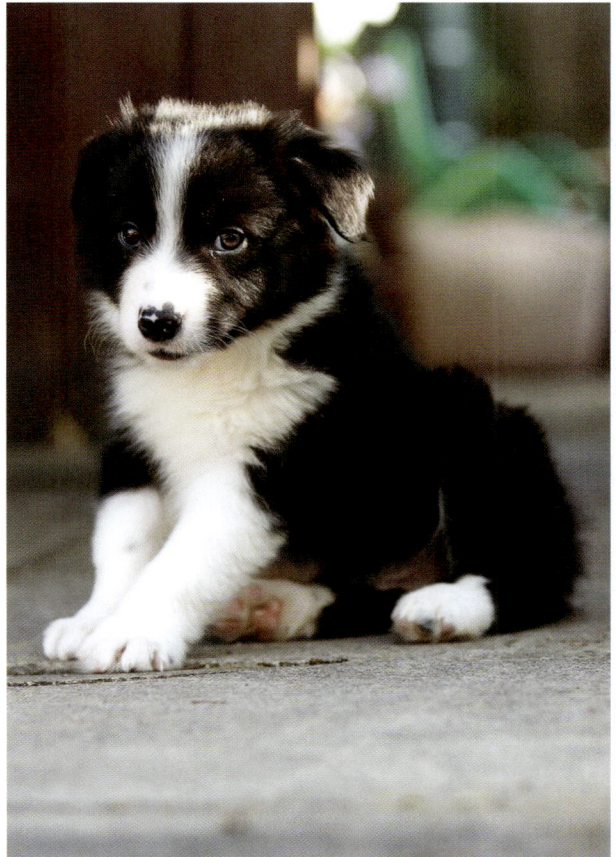

A little puppy starting out in his new life: everything is new and sometimes scary.

Puppies grow quickly, and the shy puppy soon becomes the explorer wanting to find out about everything in sight – and at this stage you may not notice that he is starting to push the boundaries.

him with a place of his own where he can rest and feel safe. Try not to overwhelm him, as he needs to be able to process everything he can see, and the sooner he can do that, the sooner he will start to feel at home. If you decide against a den and instead provide him with a dog bed, he may appear to be settled and happy to begin with. But once he starts to feel more confident he won't always want to stay in the bed, and because he has a lot of freedom, he just might decide for himself which places in your home he will have as his toilet area. How are you

going to handle this, and how are you going to manage him if he also decides there are several nice things in your home he would like to chew?

For a moment let's get inside his head. He is used to a small space, snuggled up with his siblings and close to the warmth of his mum. You will rarely, if ever, see a young puppy on his own lying out in the open, fully exposed to the elements and any danger that may be lurking. This comes when the puppy feels safe, which means the number one priority is to provide your pup with what he can recognize as being safe, so he can relax. Your instinct will be to hold him close to protect him, so it doesn't make sense to then put him in a large bed with no visible security. In a den he can have the warmth of a cosy bed and he can be sheltered on all sides, so the only area he needs to be concerned about is straight in front of him. You can also put paper or puppy pads in the den so he has his own complete apartment.

I have always found music to have a wonderful calming effect on both dogs and puppies – as long as it's gentle and not heavy band music!

If your pup has the run of the house he will see each room as a different area, and to him it will make sense to sleep in one and then toilet in another. You can scrub to your heart's content, but your pup will still be able to smell where he went. Every puppy and every home is different: some people will keep getting up during the night to take their pup out to try and encourage early toilet training, while others will provide a night-time area for the puppy to use, and will encourage toilet training during the day. Neither way is wrong or right, but striking a happy medium is important, as too much pressure the first way could cause the puppy to always want to be up in the night, and the second way could discourage it from trying to be clean.

Most puppies house train quite soon, but they can only work on the information we give them. If your puppy has a den, then he will soon work out that he has an area for sleeping and an area for toileting. If he is taken out regularly, especially just after a meal, he will soon stop

When a collie reaches six months the cute puppy becomes an adolescent who will push the boundaries even more; but if it is well mannered, a collie will know when not to push.

Young Dogs in Rescue

A high percentage of the dogs in the rescue are between the ages of nine and eighteen months old, and from homes where they have had everything given to them as puppies. They have had an abundance of toys, games, treats and lots of attention, but very little in the way of good manners – so when the dog begins to get wilful and wanting more and more of its own way, and it's no longer a cute little lovable bundle, it comes into the rescue as an unwanted dog.

Bess was four months old when she came into rescue. She was wilful, nipping, and constantly tugging on her lead. Teaching good manners from the very beginning can avoid this type of behaviour.

Bess was young enough to learn, and it didn't take long for her to learn to be gentle, both with others and on her lead, and to enjoy calm exercise instead of being constantly on the go.

using his indoor toilet, which will be very near his bed, as it is not in a dog's nature to soil where they live. I'm a big believer in 'if it doesn't happen, wait to give it a chance to happen'.

If your pup is one that doesn't toilet train quickly, don't worry – not all children potty train at the same age. I appreciate that if it's on your kitchen floor, or on a carpet, it can be a problem as your pup's 'deposits' get larger, which is a really good reason to think carefully about using a den. Whichever you choose and however long it takes, don't scold your pup for doing what is natural to him – just work out the best way to teach him where you want him to do it.

Early Days

As cute and lovable as your pup is, in a few short months he'll be an adolescent collie. Think ahead to how you want him to behave when he is older, because what he does as a small cute puppy, he will still expect to be allowed to do when he grows up. Imagine him on the furniture running up and down and throwing cushions on the floor as he tries to bury his head under them. As a puppy it may be entertaining, but how funny will it be when he is over six months old and he tries to take over the settee when you have visitors? If you want to change the rules with a child you can explain how and why you are changing them, but how are you going to tell your pup that what he has done for several weeks has to stop? If you move house it's easier, as a new home has new rules, but that's a rather drastic action, so instead consider starting as you would want to go on.

Try not to flood your puppy with too much information, and concentrate on the things you *really* need him to understand. This includes lead walking, and teaching commands such as 'sit', 'stay' and 'lie down' – but this is a lot of instructions for an adult dog to absorb in a short time, so for a puppy it's far too much. While he is young and wants to be with you, try teaching him the one thing that people are still often struggling with when the pup reaches adolescence – his recall. Decide what word you want to use, and every time he comes to you, say the word. He will eventually hear the word and come to you. This is subliminal training: when we are training a dog to work sheep we don't try and teach them a left and a right command, we put them round a small flock of sheep and each

time they go left or right we give them the appropriate command. But before we do that we need two basic essentials: the stop and recall, because without those we have no control over a dog.

Another important thing to understand is that because they can only take in so much at a time, they will store that information to be able to learn something else. A dog may seem to forget something when he's concentrating on learning a new instruction, but he will be able to recall it when he has absorbed the new information.

Avoid Rushing

Let your puppy enjoy his puppyhood without pressuring him. Children should enjoy their childhood, and puppies should be able to enjoy life without the pressure of a lot of training. Training for a dog should be like 'big school' for children, and their puppy months should be about learning good manners and respect. Think about what a puppy learns when he is with his mum. She isn't going to teach him to 'sit', to 'lie down', to bring a ball back or perform any tricks. He will enjoy his puppyhood playing with his siblings, or on his own amusing himself. Mum will interact with him, but he won't be allowed to nip her. His instinct at this vulnerable age will make him want to follow her when leaving the den, or going anywhere new, rather than trying to lead the way. He will have fun, but he will be respectful and well mannered. If he isn't, and decides to make his own rules, then his life could be in danger from predators.

In your home there are no predators of the wild, but every stranger, other dog or new situation can be a worry to him. If he has had a good mum your puppy will come to *you* understanding about the rules of respect and not pushing in front; he will also be perfectly capable of amusing himself. Instead of trying to teach him how to have the fun that you understand, enjoy watching him amusing himself, learn about him as he shows you how he can work things out for himself, and help him to expand his knowledge so you can share new experiences together.

Does this sound as if I'm telling you not to have fun with your pup and that you shouldn't make too much fuss of him? It's actually the opposite. Puppies are irresistible, and are just meant for cuddling and lavishing attention on, and I find it hard to believe that anyone has ever reared a puppy without making far more than

Try to see the world as your puppy sees it. A person in the room will see walls, windows, television and pictures. Your puppy will see the floor, where there will be interesting smells, and the bottom of everything that you see. This is his world.

When you pick up your puppy he can see what you see, until he looks down: *his* world has now become a floor and a pair of feet, and they are a long way down!

Don't overload your young collie with too much information, and allow him to discover his own games; collies can be very inventive when it comes to amusing themselves, and don't be offended if they sometimes prefer to be on their own.

one mistake. It's because of this that we need to set some boundaries so that the mistakes, which are inevitable, are few and are easily rectified.

Through your Puppy's Eyes

I cannot stress enough the importance of seeing the world from your dog's perspective. At some point I believe everyone who has a pup will get down on the floor to play with it, and when you do, take a moment to look around at the view your puppy has. Although you know it is seeing everything at floor level, it's hard to understand what the view really is if you don't look at it as yourself – so take a moment to almost *be* your puppy. If you can do this, you will notice things that you have previously never

A False Perspective

Most people will pick up their puppy – they may be showing him to a friend, carrying him to the car, or simply giving him a cuddle. But from down at almost floor level your puppy is now seeing the world as you see it. Puppies learn from actions, and when they are carried and handed over to other people to hold, they begin to see that it is beneficial for them to get as near to a person's shoulder or face as they can. As they grow bigger and start jumping up at strangers in order to do what they did as a puppy, they will fail to understand why suddenly this action is no longer reaping the rewards it did when they were little.

had the need to pay attention to.

First of all let's take a good look at feet. You pup is suddenly aware of pairs of feet walking around him – and then feet and legs disappear through doors. A timid pup may be worried, but a nosy parker will want to follow. Feet run, they walk, they can take big strides and small strides. A timid pup may be worried, but a more forward pup might want to chase the feet and even get hold of them to slow them down. Take another look around and you may see chair legs, doors opening and closing, and all those lovely smells. Smells are on the floor, on the passing feet, they come in on the air from the kitchen, and smells that have yet to be identified.

You may also see shoes on the floor, and at some point, a pup may feel those shoes need investigating. Footwear also has a smell that is now familiar, so why not get into that shoe a bit further, chew a bit here and a bit there, and what a busy and confusing picture for such a little being.

Then the noises: telephones, doors opening, the television and all the different voices – and all those sounds are coming from overhead. Now that you can see what he can see, you can understand just how much he has to take in, and how he really does need time to be able to adjust to each new sight and sound before you start giving him even more to think about.

One thing I would beg you to think very carefully

about is this: a puppy follows its mother everywhere, it doesn't tell her when and where to go, it isn't born taking over leadership and it isn't mature enough to take control, so pulling on a lead isn't something it would naturally do. When your pup is feeling confident and runs ahead of you from room to room, every so often call him back and walk through in front of him. When going out into the garden, don't take the easy route of letting him run out as soon as the door is open: either step outside first, or stand in front of him and then move so he can go out. Put a light lead on him and let him get used to it before you start leading him with it – and when you do, keep everything gentle and calm. If you have encouraged him to follow rather than to go in front, you will find him very easy to lead train.

Take a journey inside your puppy's head for a moment and see it from his point of view. If he sees you about to move to another room, he will anticipate your move and run ahead of you. To us, he is showing how bright he is, but for him, *he* is taking you to that room. When you open the door to go into the garden and he runs straight out in front of you, he is seeing an open door and instant freedom, and once over the threshold he is in control.

This may not seem an issue when he is a small puppy, but when he is a full grown adolescent dog and wanting to test the boundaries, he will already think he is in control. He will be much harder to hold, and it will be even more difficult to stop him from pulling on the lead. For a moment, keep inside his head and then ask yourself the question that *he* would ask, could he speak: 'Why are you struggling to keep up with me, and why are you getting upset? This is what you allowed me to do as a puppy, and therefore *you* taught me to behave like this.' There will be so many things that you won't want your dog to do, but will inadvertently teach it to do, that taking a little longer to set the boundaries at the beginning will pay dividends as he grows up.

Summary

Don't confuse your puppy with too much information too soon: allow him time to settle down, and from the start encourage him to want to be with you, not because you have treats or toys, but because you are creating a bond of love. While it's fine for him to go to other people, don't overdo it, and make sure that he goes from you with your permission, and comes back to you. This will not make him nervous of strangers, on the contrary, it will make him feel secure and safe with you. Would you let a five-year-old child go up to strangers? Or allow strangers to approach that child? You need to give the same protec- tion to your puppy or adult dog that you would to a child. This doesn't make children nervous of strangers, it allows them to grow up feeling safe while they learn to make their own judgements.

CHAPTER 10

A Rescue Dog in your Home

The definition of the word 'rescue,' according to various dictionaries, is 'to help someone or something out of a dangerous, harmful, or unpleasant situation'. If you take in a dog from a friend, or if you buy a dog, technically you are not rescuing it, even if you get your dog from a rescue centre. They have rescued it and you are adopting it. So before we begin to settle this dog into your home, I want to delve a little into the term 'rescue' and what it means, not to you, but to your dog.

There are many reasons why people want to rehome their dog. Some will be genuine, but many are trying to move on a dog that has issues they can no longer cope with. Some ask for money to avoid enquiries from disreputable people and dealers, but some simply want to make money. Some offer their dogs as 'free to a good home', and while this states they genuinely want a good home, they don't realize that putting a price, no matter how small, on their pet may help to safeguard it. From any of those sources you are on your own, there is unlikely to be any backup if you are struggling, and if the dog has issues it is equally unlikely that the person who sold or gave it to you will take it back. Or you may have gone to one of the many rescue centres where, if it's a reputable and conscientious establishment, you will receive information about your dog, and you will have some backup.

There is one thing that every one of the dogs described in the sidebar overleaf has in common, and that is, they have all been rejected, and in most cases are unwanted and unloved. I say 'most cases' because there are genuine cases where the dog is being rehomed because it is loved (*see box* 'A Tale of Three Dogs').

You must also consider that if there is nobody to take in an unwanted dog, then sometimes heartbreaking decisions are the only option. It's easy for people to say they would never do this, but we would also want was best for our dogs.

I know that people working in rescue centres are often hurt when they hear someone say they 'rescued' the dog from them, when in fact they adopted the dog from the rescue. I have struggled with the correct word to use in this chapter, so I thought of the words I don't like using and eliminated them. I don't like the word 'owner': we don't own our children, we are their parents, and if we take on a child from a home that has no family, we adopt them.

Border Collies are free spirits, and we either have them from puppies, or we take them on as young or older adults; just like children, they are either with us from the beginning, or they are adopted. Whether from a friend, 'free to a good home', purchased, or from a rescue centre, you have adopted the dog into your life, and when you take on that responsibility you are not just providing a loving home, you become its guardian, its protector and its mentor. It is not an easy road to walk, but when you put in the work, you will be rewarded with your dog taking you into its heart:

Taking a dog into your life is like a marriage: you have to get to know each other and you have to work at the relationship, but for better or worse it should be for life.

A Tale of Three Dogs

Cap as an elderly, retired working collie; he belonged to a farmer who was worried about his dog's future.

The farmer who asked us to take Cap, an elderly retired working dog, into rescue was worried about what would happen to his dog if anything happened to him: with no one to give Cap a home, he feared his old dog would end up in a dog pound. He is now in retirement and is his guardian's best friend.

Sam was two years old, and the young shepherdess who brought him in cried as she left him, but he didn't want to work so he was left at home all day while she worked. She knew there was a better life for him.

Ben was six years old when his elderly carer began to lose his sight and knew he would eventually have to go into a home – so rather than wait until that day came, he made arrangements for his dog to come into rescue.

Were they selfish, or did they perform an act of love? They all cried, but they knew that the dogs would be well looked after and would eventually be rehomed and have good lives.

For whatever reason a dog is in rescue, they all have one thing in common: they have all been rejected, and it takes time for them to settle down to new faces and new routines.

A very nervous or sensitive dog may turn away from you if you try to make eye contact. A collie controls with his eyes, and to stare at him can be quite threatening. Never try to force eye contact with a collie: they will seek to make eye contact with someone as they learn to trust them.

An adult dog can bring with him bad habits, or even fear from his past. He has no reason to trust you, so you need to be patient and earn his trust, but this is made easier with a knowledge of the breed. This dog has blue eyes, not a very short coat, drop ears and is tri-merle: this means he is sensitive, stubborn, and doesn't crave attention. He needs to be allowed plenty of time to learn to trust.

Through your Dog's Eyes

For the rest of this chapter I will refer to the older or rescued dog as 'adopted'. Although there are various ways the dog can come into your life, there is always one defining factor, abandonment, and this includes the dog that has previously been in a loving home. Let us take a moment to see his life from his point of view: one day he was somewhere he believed to be his world – whether it was good, bad, happy or unhappy, it was all he knew. Then suddenly he is taken from it, and is somewhere completely new and with people he doesn't really know. Only if you have known the dog before you adopted him are you familiar, and even then, not as a permanent part of his life.

You may have the first few days planned, and you know how you want your own and your dog's life to be, but tomorrow doesn't exist for your dog: all he knows is the uncertainty and confusion of today. Why should he trust you, and how is he to understand what you want of him? You may know his name, and you may even know some of the words he has previously been used to, but do you have the same tone of voice, and do you pronounce the words in the accent and the tone he is used to hearing?

For the first few days keep your dog on a long line in the garden: this not only ensures that you can catch him, but it will prevent him from jumping out.

Dogs Recognize Accents and Tones

When training a dog to work sheep, we emphasize the first letter of the left and right commands: away to the right and come-bye to the left. This means that should the shepherd be from a different county, or from Wales, or Scotland, the first letter will be recognized by the dog. The rest of the word will then be recognized by tone, and he will soon learn to recognize the tone as a directional sound. This helps to reduce any possible confusion, and because the dog knows the shepherd, he will already be used to his voice.

The Older Dog

Settling in an older dog refers to any dog that is no longer a puppy, though it is not dissimilar to having a new puppy. Obviously there will be some things that don't apply, as the older dog is not coming to you straight from his mother and his siblings. However, he is still coming into a different home, with new smells, new people and different sounds. If you know very little about the dog or his background, allowing him time to settle and to adjust is vital for him.

Any dog, young or old, needs to be able to observe and to work out his place in the home. Take a moment to get down on the floor and have a good look at what your new dog is seeing. He may have come from a home that was

open plan, and you may have several rooms; he may have been used to sitting on the furniture or going upstairs; he may have been in a shed or a barn. His actions will tell you what he is used to doing, so show him patience, try to listen to what he is telling you, and guide him to what you want him to do, rather than expecting him to understand. Collies are amazing, but when they are stressed and uncertain, reading the mind of someone who is almost a stranger is not something you can take for granted they will be able to do!

At the top of your list of things to do and places to go to, you need to write in capital letters: 'I must give my dog time to understand me, and I must accept this can take weeks or even months.' Notice that I say 'I must give my dog time to understand me'. You know you need to understand your dog, and you will be working hard to achieve this, but your dog isn't aware of a need to understand you. Never forget that taking this dog into your life was your choice, but your dog was never given a choice from the day he left his mother. He may have bonded, or not bonded, with certain people, but the freedom to choose where he lived was never his.

It's never simply a question of us understanding the dog: we know we want to do that, but we have to work hard at persuading a dog to want to understand us. To rush your dog could cause him to be distrustful, and that can set you back to the first day you brought him home, because you will have to start all over again.

Whatever the age of your new dog, provide a safe

When a nervous or previously abused dog starts to pull on a lead the 'panic button' is activated and it just wants to run.

Never try to bring this dog back to you – instead, walk towards it using the lead to prevent it from moving forwards, gently stroke it, but don't bend over its face.

Always work in the same area, and your dog will eventually relax; he may not want to look at you yet, but it's a step forward.

place for him to rest and feel safe. When you feed him, leave him alone to eat in peace, and give him time. He will eventually feel curious and want to investigate, but it must be when he is ready. If your dog is confident and with few issues or none at all, he should settle quickly, but if your dog has issues it will take a lot longer and will require even more patience.

The Problem or Rescued Dog

The most difficult and complex dogs to settle in are those that have issues; these are usually dogs adopted from rescues, and even the best and most professional establishments can only take a dog so far. A wise man once said to me, if you teach someone to swim in shallow water they will be nervous of going further, but teach them to swim in deep water and they will find the shallow water easy to negotiate. Some adopters are thrown in at the deep end, so for this section we will look mainly at the dogs with more complex or serious problems. Understanding the complexity of these dogs and their issues is also the key

Standing up and far more confident; the work is done in the same area, but even now if we look at this dog's tail we know it is still not ready for the next step.

Once your dog starts to acknowledge you, don't get ambitious and try going for a walk. There is still a long way to go.

to settling in the dogs that don't have major issues, but nevertheless have still been abandoned.

Problems can cover many different issues, such as nervousness, dominance or fear, and can be present on their own, or all together. A nervous or frightened dog can become dominant in order to protect itself, but it can also be driven to the other extent of being so scared it becomes withdrawn and tries to isolate itself. This is where everything you learned in Chapter 3 will help you to identify the character of the dog you have taken into your life. A nervous or scared tri-coloured short-coated dog may take longer to adjust than the longer-coated, black-and-white collie, but the amber-eyed collie needs a lot more personal space – and don't keep trying to make eye contact, as this will make him feel threatened. With the knowledge gained in the first chapters you will almost be able to look at your dog and know what he is thinking, what he's been through, and how to make him feel secure.

Dogs are not born with a fear of people, neither are they born aggressive or withdrawn. How they develop is down to human management, be it from cruelty, neglect or lack of knowledge. The temperament of each individual dog can influence how it reacts to situations, but at the end of the day you are dealing with a dog that has been let

Collies will jump a five-bar gate when they are working, so a garden fence rarely poses a problem. If they can peep over the top and see something interesting, they will step back and take a running jump out of your garden.

Never underestimate the spring that an older dog can get in his step if wants to break out.

down by another human being. So why should it put all its trust and faith in you? To begin with, don't lower any expectations of the progress you might achieve – instead don't have any, not because you might be disappointed if they don't work out, but because if you have expectations you will put pressure on your dog, which is the last thing he needs.

Above any feelings of anxiety, worry or concern regarding your ability to understand your dog, is the need for an overwhelming desire to love him, not to own or to control, simply to love. Following that is the realization that although love is essential, on its own it is not enough: it needs to be partnered with understanding and the implementing of boundaries. The first one is easy, but the last two take time and patience, and sometimes we can be guilty of rushing dogs before they are ready to move on.

A percentage of lost dogs have only been in their new homes for a few days. If you have ever lost sight of a dog for just a few short minutes think how you would feel if you lost your new dog. He has no idea of the area, has no familiar landmarks, and as yet doesn't even know that the home he has just run away from was full of love and security. A responsible rescue should prepare for this in their terms and conditions, but I have found that without an explanation for the necessity of those conditions, people don't always adhere to them. The Freedom of Spirit Trust for Border Collies (FOSTBC) has very strict conditions for settling in a new dog, and whilst I am sure that some adopters who adopt a relatively easy dog may not see the reason for them, once the conditions are followed, dogs settle in far more quickly and with less stress.

When you take your new dog home, don't take him straight out for a walk. He doesn't know your boundaries or see life the way you do, so if you walk him for half a mile he will believe that this is his boundary. For the first two days keep him on garden exercise only; even if he has no issues at all he will be fine in your garden, which to you may seem boring, but he's never seen it before and it will be full of new and exciting smells. Two days is not long, and it really isn't long enough. We have found that those adopters who keep to garden exercise for a bit longer have fewer issues when they do go for a walk, and they develop a good relationship with their dog far more quickly than those who rush to go out and about.

Your first walk should be a short one. You will probably know a lot of lovely walks that you would love to go on, but this isn't about you, it's about your dog and

It's lovely to see a dog running free, but if it is let off the lead too soon it may just keep running and get lost.

the relationship you are building with him. A short walk to you may be one that you take regularly and it's boring, and you want your dog out there in the fields or on the moors running and playing. But how important is what you want, compared to what your dog needs, and his safety? We may walk down the lane and across the fields with the dogs in our rescue every day, but to a new dog the garden is amazing, and when the time comes for a short walk they are inundated with new smells and new things to look at. When they have done that a few

The human eye sees the path, the trees, the gate ahead and the grass beyond the gate.

The dog sees the grass, which will have lots of lovely smells, the shadow that keeps moving, and the gate if he looks ahead, but he cannot see beyond the gate. Anyone coming through that gate can take him by surprise.

times we have had the opportunity to learn more about them, and in turn they have started to listen to us. It is a few short days to us, but to them it's a totally new experience. So keep the walks short to begin with, and instruct all well meaning friends not to visit for a few weeks.

Part of the terms and conditions for the FOSTBC-adopted dogs are garden exercise for a minimum of two days, a lead or long training line for a minimum of eight weeks, no visitors for at least two weeks, and put the toy box away. This works, as we are looking at adoption from the dog's point of view, and not the adopters. How can a dog work out who lives in the home, and who is he to turn to if there are several people visiting and giving him attention? He needs to learn about your home and your rules, but if there are a lot of distractions, and if that includes lots of toys, he will struggle to listen to you.

How can he learn about his immediate surroundings if you keep taking him further afield? And how can he learn to want to be with you if you let him off the lead to run around and make his own decisions? How can he learn to concentrate on one thing if he is surrounded by toys? Would you let a toddler make their own decisions? Would you adopt a child and then let in half the neighbourhood to be involved? Would you take the child out on day one before they are settled into your home, and before they have begun to get to know you? Would you let a toddler trot off on their own a long way in front of you? No, you would be far too protective, and that same level of care and protections is owed to your dog.

Nervous Dogs

The more nervous dog can make a wonderful faithful friend, but you need to be prepared to give them space and a lot of time. If they want to sit in a corner and observe, let them do it. For them it's a learning curve, and until they feel they can trust you, they will feel safer in a den or a corner just watching. Trying to tempt them out with treats or toys might seem logical to the human mind, but to a collie who doesn't understand either of them, you are making it suspicious of you.

Don't feel sorry for the dog that doesn't understand a ball. Instead of trying to get him to play with a ball, and most nervous dogs will be scared of it, wait until he has more confidence and then find out what he wants to play, and how. If two people move in together they don't just settle into a new routine overnight: it takes time and

Your dog may not be very tactile, and he may not want to meet your gaze, but you can still share quality time. Don't bend over him and don't try to 'face-to-face' with him. Keep upright and stand behind him, and then gently massage his shoulders. This dog hasn't learned to accept people in his space, but like this he has a clear space in front of him so he doesn't feel threatened and is learning to enjoy the experience.

patience and a lot of give and take, and maybe a few arguments along the way. Yet so many times people expect a dog that didn't ask to live with them, doesn't understand what is happening, and can't understand the new words, to move in and settle into their way of life and routine quickly: in fact they need months.

It takes three weeks before a dog begins to really relax, and for a nervous dog, the more you rush, the longer it will take. It's another three months before you begin to understand each other, and after a year most people realize that when they thought they knew their dog at six months, it actually took a year.

House Training

You may be lucky and your dog may be clean from day one, but most dogs, even clean ones, can have a toilet accident for a few nights. Let's look at it from their point of view: wherever they have come from they will have had their own 'spot' for toileting – it may have been outside or in the corner of a shed or a kennel, and now they are in completely different surroundings. You may have had a dog previously, in which case there will be the scent of another dog in your home, which may cause the new dog a temptation to leave a urinary 'mark'.

Outside is where you want your dog to go, but he doesn't know that. Never scold a dog for an 'accident' – rather, calmly put a lead on and take him outside to the garden; sometimes it helps to pick up what he has done in the house and put it in the garden. Collies are intelligent and pick up what you want very quickly, but you have to communicate what you want very simply and calmly. A nervous or scared dog may take a long time to be brave enough to go outside, in which case, a den with an area to toilet in will help to keep any smells from your floor, as once marked the dog will want to continue to 'go' in the same spot.

A warm utility room that is not a walk-through and where he can feel secure can be good for him to have some safe quiet time where he doesn't feel threatened by people, telephones, televisions, cookers, and all scary household noises.

Confident Dogs

I have made little reference to the stronger or dominant dog in this chapter, as any issues from this collie will be covered in a later chapter. However, despite any wish he may have to take over your home, his settling-in time is no different from the more sensitive or nervous dog, but for different reasons. Jumping up, getting on the furniture, being possessive, barking at strangers or other dogs, are not problems you can deal with in the first few weeks. You need to get to know him, and to figure out why his behaviour is so wayward. Has he been allowed or encouraged to do these things, has anyone previously tried to teach him good manners, does he bark from fear, and if so, what is he frightened of?

If his behaviour is not from fear, then he has a will to be in control, and I can guarantee he will pull on a lead, his recall will be on his terms, and he will perceive the whole house to be his. If he has a really shiny coat and doesn't carry any weight he has probably been on a high energy diet. He needs a place of his own in your home, preferably a den, and garden exercise where you can also practise getting him to walk nicely on a lead – if he pulls you on the first walk he will assume that that is the way he can

It's a wonderful moment when a dog that has had issues snuggles up to you, not because of food or gifts but because of the best gift you can share – love.

always take you for a walk. Whereas with the nervous dog you need to time to build up his trust, with the overly confident dog you need time to teach him his boundaries.

Summary

Wherever your new dog comes from, and no matter what age, remember that first and foremost it is a dog. Its instincts, its senses, everything it knows is about being a dog. Understanding that your dog is very young, is nervous, is confident, or has been abused, isn't enough: you have to understand how your dog feels, and why. If you can see the world through his eyes for even a short time you will understand his need for a safe place, and for time to adjust. Taking a dog into your life isn't easy, and sometimes it's hard work, but the harder you work, the more you will understand, and the more you will achieve.

You know that you are going to give your rescue dog a loving home, but he doesn't understand that. He just knows he's being moved on yet again. He needs time to settle in, and just as we need time to get to know new people, he needs you to provide him with some space and plenty of patience so he can get to know you at his own pace.

CHAPTER 11

Border Collies with Children

I can remember when any choices in life were quite simple: you either ate out or ate at home, there was nowhere to drive through or to drive in, and the only 'takeaway' was fish and chips. You had a good book or you watched television, and if you wanted to do something special you went to the cinema. Now it's possible to watch a film in your home while your food is delivered, having had lunch at a drive-through. Why am I talking about the past when we have it so good now, with so much freedom and so many choices? Because when there was little choice it was far less confusing than having to weigh up all the choices we have today: there is so much information available now that which film to go to, whether to eat in or out, and which drive-through to choose, can become a problem when each one is claiming to be the best.

Too Much Information

Before the advent of websites, social media, blogs, vlogs and training aids, the requirements needed when you got a dog were a lead, a bed, a feed bowl, a water dish, and a good pair of walking shoes. We now have all this wonderful information at our fingertips – literally. Just type 'I have a new Border Collie' into a search engine on the internet and you will get so much information that your head will spin. But this breed has changed very little in over 200 years, so why would it have changed in the last thirty years? The short answer is that it hasn't, and nor have we, but the information available has changed.

You will see advertisements on television describing

A lovely relationship can evolve with collies and children, but it needs sensible parenting, well mannered children and the right dog – and it is still hard work and a lot of preparation.

how putting one drop of a wonder solution lifts caked grease off a cooker, and stains several years old from a carpet. In reality we all know that it will take more than

Should you have a Border Collie? A positive answer would require knowing about the background and behaviour of these two dogs, but learning from the early chapters, can you decide which would be the best candidate if you were thinking of adding a dog into your family and you have children?

cream to do it, even if it appears to be a super duper world beater on the screen. It's called marketing, and you will find information about your dog that requires you to spend money on items you don't need, and there will be pages of information about how your collie will nip children because it nips sheep, and how it will round them up and herd them into a corner. I fail to see the connection between sheep and children, particularly as children on farms have grown up with collies – and still do – without having problems, and both know what a sheep is. I have heard it said that a person 'can't have too much information' – but if a lot of the information is contradictory, or is not from an experienced source, it can do more harm than good.

If you have young children, getting a puppy might seem a good choice because it 'will grow up with the kids'. But a puppy isn't a child and it can be hard work, and in a busy home it might not get the input it needs. It will get a lot of attention and playtime, but sometimes the time needed to educate the puppy isn't always available. With just one child, a parent at home all day, and the investment of common sense, time and patience, then a wonderful friendship between dog and child can be nurtured. But more than one young child, a busy home, or

never having had a puppy or a collie before, are all factors to be taken into account. Puppies are amazing, they are cuddly, loving, lovable little souls, and they are very hard to resist, but at six months they have grown into what in our human world we call 'the terrible teens'. And if they reach that age with problems, those problems are likely to multiply.

If you are going for an older dog, take heed of the information in Chapter 3 about colour genes, coat and eye colour. You may fall in love with a collie that fits your criteria, but if it isn't going to fit into your family's life, then you must wait until you find the dog that is right for the family.

Should You Have a Collie?

I grew up with collies and so did most of my friends, so it would be hypocritical to say people with children shouldn't have one. But I have also lost count of the number of collies in rescue because they were 'nippy' with the children, and in some cases had bitten them. But we have to see the world as the dog sees it, and we need to get inside his head and understand why he does what he does. Only then can someone decide if they can make it work or not.

Collies are intelligent and sensitive; they are quick to learn and often slow to forget. If a child does something you disapprove of, you can explain why you disapprove, but if a dog does something you disapprove of, you don't have the luxury of a verbal explanation. If we make a mistake, we accept it, and hopefully will learn from it, but a dog doesn't make mistakes. It has no right or wrong; it responds to what life offers it, and once it has done something it will see no reason why it can't do it again.

The dog will base its actions on whether something causes pleasure or pain. If the after effect of the action is pain (for example, if a dog jumps over a wall and hurts itself on landing it will learn that jumping walls can cause pain), it will try to avoid that feeling in the future. A dog's pleasure can be derived from *our* actions towards it, such as praise, reward, massaging, but it also comes with excite-

ment. Being excited at going out for a walk or being fed is a controllable excitement, but when a collie is playing with other dogs or children and is racing around, it becomes overexcited. Once overexcited, the dog will be really enjoying the hyperactive state it is in, and it will try to instigate the games and the feeling again. However, overexcitement can lead to agitation and to unwanted behaviour.

At this point, to give you a little more insight into how the dog sees the world, I feel I need to mention that the dog that felt pain from jumping the wall is likely to be wary of other walls. It may seem strange to the dog's guardian when they are trying to negotiate a style in a stone wall that their dog doesn't want to climb it, but the wall can trigger a memory that tells the dog he needs to keep away from it. He won't know why, but he will have a feeling of fear, and he will respond to it by keeping away from it. We will cover a dog's memory bank in a later chapter.

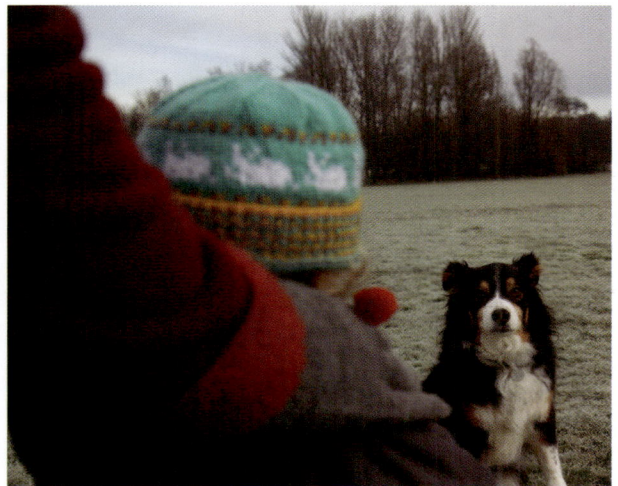

A collie is on the same eye level as a child, which can mean the dog feels threatened or has a desire to control. Sensible parenting and training are essential for the dog to feel secure.

A collie must look upwards to an adult, which means that close up they are not on the same eye level.

Two young dogs playing and having fun: they will play wrestle, and will often growl and even use their teeth. Puppies and young dogs need to be taught not to see children as their siblings.

Controlling Movement

Collies are bred to control movement, and we need to understand to what degree they need to exert control, and what they are prepared to do to maintain it. A wide belief is that collies nip because that's what they do with sheep, but it's about control, not chase, and they only do what is needed and in a controlled way. For example, take one sheep running away from the flock and the dog tries to head it off: he can't pass the sheep in order to control it with his body, so he will jump at its side and grab its wool. He does this in an effort to make the sheep turn, or to slow it down so the shepherd can catch it. If the dog doesn't do his job the sheep can end up lost or causing an accident.

The working dog has been trained not just to do his job, but to respond to emergency situations with a calm authority: once he has the sheep secured he will go back to doing his job as usual. He won't go round trying to bite other sheep, and neither will he become an aggressive dog. Don't get me wrong, I love this breed and everything about them, but they are passionate and often obsessive about what they do. If you watch a sheepdog trial and some of the sheep are being really awkward, especially at the pen, you may see a dog 'grip' the wayward sheep – he will also be disqualified for doing it. But in a work situation he would have had more freedom to control the sheep. He wouldn't have been taking them through gates with no walls, and he wouldn't have kept receiving commands from the shepherd that restricted his freedom to make decisions, so quite simply he lost his temper.

Now put a dog with all those capabilities in a home with children running around, and a lot of energy and noise in the air, and with no training on how to harness his instincts, and you can see where it can go wrong.

What a Puppy Sees

Puppies will run and play together, they will enjoy play fighting, and this may include nipping, but it will only be with siblings. If they participate in play with their mother or older dogs and they nip, they will be put firmly in their place, usually with a reciprocal but much firmer nip. I know there is a chain of thought that if a pup bites you, biting its ear will teach it a lesson – but I would strongly

When children get wound up they will often lash out, and when dogs get wound up they often bite. Notice the older dog in the background just about to come in and separate them. Good parenting is essential to keep things calm.

The two dogs shown in the previous photo are still best friends, but it doesn't always work out that way with a dog and a child. Two young dogs learn by testing each other, but a child and a dog are not the same, so both need to learn how to interact with each other in a calm way.

recommend that you don't do it. For one thing, you are not a dog, nor did you give birth to the pup, and biting it for doing something it thought it was all right to do is not the way forwards.

Getting a new puppy is exciting for children, but so is going to the seaside – but you wouldn't leave them on the beach unattended, and you wouldn't let them wander into the sea. But what harm is there in letting them play with the new puppy, and allowing them to pick it up and carry it around? What they do with the puppy at the beginning they won't be able to do when it's a fully grown dog – they won't be able to pick it up and carry it around, and they won't be able to outrun it in a game of chase. So they have changed, but the pup, now a fully grown dog, hasn't, and will still think it can do the things it did as a puppy.

When children are running around the puppy sees the movement, and like all good collie pups, he is on a mission to control that movement. He will probably have played similar games with his siblings, but he doesn't yet know how to control this urge, and he is very excited, so he nips. Children may react with a squeal or a scream and the puppy will usually have one of two possible reactions: he will either shrink away in fear, or he will get more excited by the noise on his sensitive ears, and will try even more to take control.

To understand the puppy and to prevent this from happening, we must first ask, what did he do wrong? As far as the parents are concerned, the puppy bit their child and they are worried that it may happen again, and the child is now probably nervous of the pup. But the pup did what is natural to him: he didn't intend to hurt anyone, he simply followed his instincts, and at his tender age the instincts are fun. He didn't start the game, he simply joined in, and played the only way he knew how. Preventing this is where the hard work is: the puppy is not a playmate for the children, they are not his siblings, and the time when children and puppy are together should be limited, supervised and educational.

If a child is considered too young to learn how to respect a dog, and a parent hasn't time to supervise them, then please consider waiting for a few more years. But with time and patience a child can learn how to be gentle, how to be considerate, and how to respect all animals, and how to have a best friend without winding them up. A puppy doesn't know anything of house rules, and doesn't understand that children are not playmates to play chase with – but neither does he have a preconceived idea of what to expect, because, unlike an older dog, he's not been in a home situation before. From the first day into your home and your life, make sure you show him what you want, and steer him away from what you don't want.

A baby gate is marvellous, but if you rely on it as a tool to separate dog and child you will find that as soon as the gate is opened, the dog will rush through. There will be times when the gate is open, so teach your dog to wait before going through.

For a moment let us reverse the situation and imagine that you are in a dog's natural environment. You are with a small pack of dogs living in the wild; you have no idea what is expected of you, and you have no rules to follow. You see food on the floor and eat some, and the other young dogs don't stop you – they even start to approach, and they let you join in their games. Then one day, one of the dogs hurts you and you lash out at it, and from that moment on you are no longer welcome and you don't feel safe any more. Isn't that what happens when a puppy or an older dog joins in the games before they are taught any rules?

But caution would have made you stand back and observe, and find out about any rules. Your puppy or new dog understands this, but our nature is to include them immediately, which puts the newcomer into an excitable position since there are no rules or parenting.

Prepare your Dog for a New Baby

Dogs really need preparing for the huge event of a new baby. It can come as quite a shock to them when one day life is normal, and a few days later there is a noisy, smelly, mini human in the home and 'normal' has disappeared. The usual routine doesn't seem to exist any more, and everyone's time and attention seems to be spent on the newcomer. There are nine months available to prepare a dog for the changes that are going to be in his life, and the sooner you start, the better and easier it will be for your dog.

The Chill Mat

A simple piece of vet bed can be one of the biggest assets imaginable in teaching a dog how to be calm, and when not to interfere. It isn't a bed, it isn't a 'naughty step' and it doesn't stay on the floor: it is alternative behaviour. We would say to a child, 'stop running and sit down quietly'; or 'Don't play with that noisy toy, sit and read a book'; or 'Don't draw on the wall, draw on this paper.' But with a dog we tend just to tell it to stop – it may be a firm 'no', or even 'get down', but we don't always tell it what to do instead.

From the dog's point of view, if he stops doing something when you tell him to, it is only a temporary hitch. If he is told to get off the settee and he does, what should he

The Chill Mat is invaluable: here Molly is learning that she has a mat of her own, and that the other mat is not hers, and neither are the toys on it hers.

do next? If no more instruction is given, he has done as he was told and got off – but nobody said he couldn't get back on again, so the whole scenario is repeated, with both dog and guardian getting frustrated. But if the Chill Mat is put on the floor, the dog then has an alternative behaviour.

If a dog is given a treat or a toy, or is told he is a good dog when he gets off the settee, in his eyes he is being rewarded for being on the settee. His mind has received a message of getting on the settee, and getting off earns a reward. Dogs will always remember the last action, and in this instance the settee and the reward are one memory. However, if the dog is asked to get off the settee and is guided to the Chill Mat (alternative behaviour), and he settles down on the mat and is *then* rewarded, his memory of the reward is the mat and not the settee. A reward doesn't need to be a treat or an object – the best reward for a collie is for you to sit and spend time with him, and to gently stroke or massage him. His memory then is of how lovely it is to spend time with his guardian.

You can't teach a dog two things at once, so the first thing your dog needs to learn is how to relax. Put the mat on the floor by your feet, put a lead on your dog, then sit down and relax. On a lead your dog's options are greatly reduced: you don't need to tell him what to do, because if he argues with you then you have lost the idea of him being calm. Instead, stand him on the mat and stroke or massage him. Get a cup of tea or a glass of wine and sit back in your chair and relax. If *you* don't, then *he* won't! When he's relaxed, let go of the lead and when he eventually leaves the mat, pick it up. This is the pattern for him to learn what to do: he sees the mat put on the floor, and

Digby and the Television

Digby used to try to 'chase' things on the television – he wanted to control the movement, but he had to learn that sometimes he had to ignore it. For two evenings Digby sat on the mat with his lead on. I put my foot on the lead so he couldn't move forwards, and each time he tried to move he was told to stay where he was, and that he was a good boy. He didn't get the chance to do anything that was wrong, and he was praised for keeping still. Prevention was better than any cure, and after two evenings of consistency, he chose to lie at my feet and watch the television from a distance without trying to 'chase' things and control the movement. Digby was deaf, so everything was done with hand signals – and sometimes actions really *can* speak louder than words.

that triggers a 'happy' memory for him. If he only stands on the mat to begin with, don't worry, because in time he will choose to lie down on it. It is important that he sees someone put the mat on the floor, as this is the indication he has to settle down, rather like the 'quiet cushion' for a small child. This is a very gentle and quiet time for a dog, and it should never be made stressful or confrontational.

Molly is happy on her own mat: she has learned the rules, and is happy to be included, and to stay away from the mat that is not hers. It's never too soon to start teaching a baby not to go to the dog on the mat.

A New Routine

Without a child in the home a dog will be used to being the centre of attention, and this will change when the baby is born. Feeding, nappy changing, crying, baby toys and visitors, all of this will be new, so change your dog's routine as soon as possible. When a baby has a crying time, and they all do, your dog is best either in a quiet room in the home or out on a walk with a family member. Get him used to spending some time on his own, starting with very short sessions at a time, and if he is used to being walked with two people, begin taking him out with just one of them separately once or twice a week.

Put a sheet down on the floor in your room, and put the Chill Mat down away from the sheet. Teach your dog not to go on the sheet, and to sit calmly on his mat. If you put a lead on your dog each time he goes to the sheet, ask him to leave it and to go and sit on his mat. Collies are very quick to learn, and he will soon pick up the idea as long as you don't let him get on the sheet in order to investigate it. Next put a selection of baby toys on the sheet – I'm hoping by now you can see where this is going. If he is not allowed on the sheet, then he can't have the toys: he must learn that they are not his, they belong to the sheet.

If we look into the future, at some time a toddler will be sat on the sheet playing, and may have a tantrum, or try to crawl off the sheet. If your dog is in the room at the time it will be stressful for him, and you have yet to teach the toddler to leave the dog alone. So teach your dog not just to sit on the mat, but also to leave the room when asked. If he has an instruction to go to his bed you could use that, but always make sure that he understands that he is not being told off, and praise him for being so good.

Walking with a Pram

Walking with you while you are pushing a pram will be a completely new experience for your dog, and it can be alarming. Suddenly he has wheels trundling along with him and he can't get away from them – he doesn't know if they are going to keep a distance from him, or if they are going to touch him. He won't understand that you are guiding it, or that it's not going to be a threat to him. It's better for your dog to get used to this while the pram is empty, and not when there is a baby in it.

If your dog isn't good on a lead, then lead training is essential (lead training is covered in Chapter 13). If he is used to pulling you forwards, he will start to try to do

Dogs often get less exercise when a baby arrives because they pull on the lead. Molly was already good on a lead, but needed to be taught how to walk with a pram, and not to worry about the pram wheels.

When a dog walks very close to the side of a pram their vision to one side is restricted; anyone suddenly approaching to the left of this pram would take the dog by surprise. A dog walking very near the pram can also be on the receiving end of any toys that may be thrown out.

this, and will also pull you sideways to get away from the pram. Some dogs will walk calmly at the side of a pram, but it's better to teach them to walk at your side or slightly behind you. If you look at the world from your dog's angle, you will see that if he is behind the pram he can see where it is, what is around him, and that he is also protected from anything coming towards him. At the side of the pram he is in front of you, his vision is partly blocked by the pram, and he is in the direct line of any approaching dog.

If you don't want to purchase your pram until the baby is born, try using other methods. You might feel a bit silly pushing a wheelbarrow down the road, but it's a good start to teaching your dog, and you can practise in the garden. If you know someone with a pram or a bicycle, ask if you can walk with them. Start slowly and get your dog used to standing near to the pram, and then just walk a few strides, until eventually he gets to see it as a means to a nice walk.

Educating Children

Teaching children to respect a dog is paramount: a dog is not a toy, a teddy bear, a plaything or something to keep the children company. A dog is a living being, and one that you have taken in to your life and promised to love and protect. A collie is a highly intelligent dog, with

Babies cry and scream and make a lot of high, shrill noises. This is inevitable, but the larger and more pricked up a dog's ears are, the more sensitive they will be to those high-pitched noises.

Toddlers are fascinated by eyes, but if they poke a dog in the eye it can have serious consequences. Children can learn the rules of 'do not nip or poke' when they try it on their parents. Don't wait until they try it on your dog.

keen hearing and a sensitive nature, and even if they are patient and forgiving of small hands pulling their hair, they shouldn't be put in that position. It has always amazed me when parents have told me they can't stop their child poking at the dog's eyes, pulling its tail and in general causing the dog stress and pain, enough for them to be applying for a rescue space! Yet when asked how they stop their child going near the fire or the cooker or climbing on the table, they tell me that they are always there to guide and teach it, so there is never any question of it being dangerous.

It's not just about teaching a dog how to live with children, it's essential that children are taught from day one how to live with and respect a dog. I would be telling a lie if I said it was easy: it's not. It's hard work teaching a dog, and it's hard work bringing up children, so to combine the two is going to be even more difficult. Being in control, preparing for the way forwards, being diligent, and never leaving them together unattended is a good start, and above all keep in mind that your dog is a dog, it is not a sibling to your children, and its future wellbeing and safety are dependent on you.

Summary

Be absolutely certain that you have the time for a dog. Remember that Border Collies love to control movement, so teach them how to observe, rather than interact. Don't wait until the last minute to prepare a dog for a new routine: you will know that daily life is going to change, but your dog has no idea. If your children are older and you are looking for a family dog, choose carefully, keeping the colour genes and characters in mind. If you have any doubt at all in your mind that you have either the time or the knowledge to bring a dog into your family, then my advice is – don't. Wait until you are ready – and not just one of you, but everyone in the family must be prepared for the changes that having a dog will bring. Education and training are important for your children as well as for your dog.

CHAPTER 12

Managing the Instincts

When it comes to collies I am a great believer in working with what exists, rather than trying to change them. When I was in my late teens my mum gave me some very sound advice: she told me that when it came to love, nothing was perfect, but if I tried to change someone, then they would no longer be the person I fell in love with. Instead of changing someone, or their habits, learn to manage them. She had not intended that advice for working with dogs, but that's how I interpreted it!

A Border Collie is first and foremost a sheepdog. This is its heritage; it's what over 100 years of careful breeding has proudly produced. If a dog isn't capable, mentally or physically, of working sheep, then it's not a true collie. It might not *want* to work sheep, but that's different to not being *capable* of working with them. Those that are classed as 'failed sheepdogs' (a term I hate) are often a result of a failed attempt to train them, either through lack of time or expertise – but it's usually human failure, not canine.

If a good shepherd has a true collie, and they are both capable of working with sheep, they will understand each other. If a shepherd's dog isn't a true collie then the shepherd won't be able to do his job with it. If he isn't a shepherd and his dog is a true collie, he can manage his dog's working instincts and have a wonderful companion.

Does this matter?

Understanding and managing the mind of a collie bred to work is easier than doing so with a dog that has mixed breeding in its heritage. For example, the working mind wants to control movement and is good at working out situations, but if these instincts aren't strong, a dog could try and control movement but not know why it is doing it, or what to do if it succeeds. The collie with a strong working mind is easier to understand and manage once you understand the instincts.

Controlling Movement

I love to watch a collie when it's in full stalk or stealth mode. Their bodies move with such a beautiful grace. But I also know that the stalk comes just before the action to apprehend, so as beautiful as it is to watch, it needs to be controlled. Puppies and young dogs practise their stalking techniques on each other. It will all be done in play, but the more proficient they become, the harder they will play. Watching puppies 'play' stalk is lovely, but they soon grow into adult dogs, and the fun part of the stalk turns

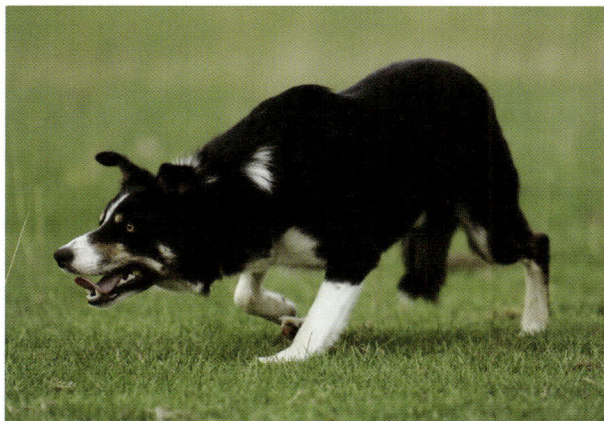

Collies are beautiful when they are stalking – they almost seem to be on tiptoe, but they are usually stalking with an intent to take action.

into something with more intent. It is part of a collie's make-up to want to stalk, but it doesn't have to take the stalk to the level of controlling. A working dog will stalk sheep in order to control them, but it is trained to stalk and control, not to stalk and attack.

If a puppy or an older dog is stalking a ball, enjoy watching the movement. But before he leaps at the ball, stop him, and call him back to you. Don't wait until he is about to leap, but call him before he becomes so engrossed that he won't hear you – you can always let him go back to it afterwards. You are teaching him that he can watch movement, but he can't always act on it.

You will be able to work out by now which of these collies you think is the most likely to be reactive to movement and will want to control cars, wheelbarrows and even the cat! Will it be the longer-coated black-and-white one, or the shorter-coated tri-coloured dog who likes to work close to the ground?

Developing Instincts Slowly

Jan and Bess were litter sisters from a working line, and both went into companion homes. Jan had toys and chased after balls. Her guardians loved to see her 'stalking' everything that moved. But by the time she was six months old she was a problem dog, chasing anything that moved. Bess played with a ball, but wasn't encouraged to chase after it. Instead, she invented her own games. When she stalked movement, her guardians loved to see it but would call her back to them. At six months Bess was not a problem dog. Kim, a third litter sister, stayed on the farm, and when she stalked the sheep in the field she was encouraged to do so because she was going to be trained to work them; however, she was discouraged from stalking the hens. At six months Kim knew where and when to direct her instincts.

Wheelbarrows, hosepipes, bicycles, cars and runners can all be targets for collies if they have not been taught to control their skills. You may be reading this chapter and thinking that you know a dog that has stalked and chased a ball, but it's never been a problem – but I would ask what colour and coat texture is that dog? And what colour are his eyes? Knowing your collie is to know how he will react to certain situations. The dogs that come in to rescue with obsessive or chase problems, and the dogs

brought for behavioural consultations, often have one, or all, of the short-coated, prick-eared, tri-coated, amber-eyed genes in common. The problems are not theirs, they are ours. We learned in the previous chapter that dogs don't make mistakes: they act on the information given, either from their instincts, or from their guardians. If stalking and chasing balls is encouraged, then in their minds they have been given the green light to stalk and chase anything that is moving.

If this dog hadn't been taught how to manage its instincts, and if it had been allowed to chase things, the lives of the ducks would be in danger. If a dog isn't taught to control its instincts, imagine how it would react if instead of ducks this was a group of children running around.

If a dog bites the vacuum or the barrow wheel, he is acting on his instinct to stop the movement. The noise of the vacuum will wind him up, and this may be accompanied by his guardian shouting at him to stop – but he won't understand why he can't try to control it. Biting the wheelbarrow may be seen as comical when he first does it, but to him, he is being told that there is a problem of movement and he has to take control. If he can't round it up to stop it, then he must use his teeth. Now we can see how easy it is for a collie that hasn't been taught how to control his instincts to end up in trouble.

There is a lot of movement in a home environment: the washing machine, the television, visitors are just a few examples, and if a dog is involved with all of these then he will feel committed to take control. Introducing your dog to the concept of the Chill Mat (*see* Chapter 11) will not only save time and frustration for yourself, but can explain very simply to your dog what you want of him. A collie sees life in an uncomplicated way: he realizes one action hurts, another doesn't; that this person can be trusted, but that one can't; that this action pleases people, but that one doesn't. It's very black and white to begin with, but gradually it will work out into a comfortable grey area. Problems arise when a collie is put into a grey area before learning the black and white.

Bonny and the Chill Mat

Bonny was learning to work sheep, but in the middle of a wet winter her training had to be postponed. She quickly turned her attention to the television. All that movement was fascinating, and she would sit directly in front of the screen. She didn't jump at it, she just watched, and although it was amusing and kept her happy, it was becoming an obsession. If the television had grown legs and had run out of the room, she would have chased it. Bonny was introduced to the Chill Mat. It was at my feet, and with a lead on her, she didn't have the option to stand in front of the television. After a few evenings she learned that she could sit and watch the movement from a distance, but at any attempt to join in the movement she would be told to 'leave' it (previously taught to her), and to give me her attention. Bonny is short-coated and tri-coloured, and knowing how obsessive her nature could be, I knew I had to act quickly to teach her some boundaries.

Imagine how much nicer it will be if your dog doesn't jump up at visitors, sits and watches the cat from a distance, and walks at the side of the wheelbarrow instead of trying to stop it moving.

Note that it's important that the Chill Mat only goes on the floor when it is needed, and your dog needs to see you put it down.

Memory Bank

Dogs' memories don't delve into the past, but they do have what I describe as memory triggers. There is an example in Chapter 11 of a dog that hurts itself jumping over a wall, and when it sees another wall, its memory triggers off that walls cause pain. Anything that leaves an impression will be remembered by a trigger. For example, a motor car backfiring and scaring a dog can leave a memory that cars are to be scared of. A dog may shy away from someone for what appears to be no apparent reason, but if the person in question reminds the dog of someone who has hurt him in the past, the trigger will warn him to be wary of that person. It may be their appearance, but it can also be a smell, such as deodorant, perfume, even oil.

It also works the other way round, as the memory can trigger off good memories. A dog came into rescue when her owner passed away. When she was rehomed, her guardian was puzzled when each time they saw a bench, when out walking, Jess would run up and jump on it and look really happy. They found out that in her previous home they had walked for miles and had stopped to rest each time they came across a bench. Jess's memory bank was triggered each time she saw a bench of a happy time in her past. Understanding this made it easier for her guardian to keep the memory sweet while they created new ones.

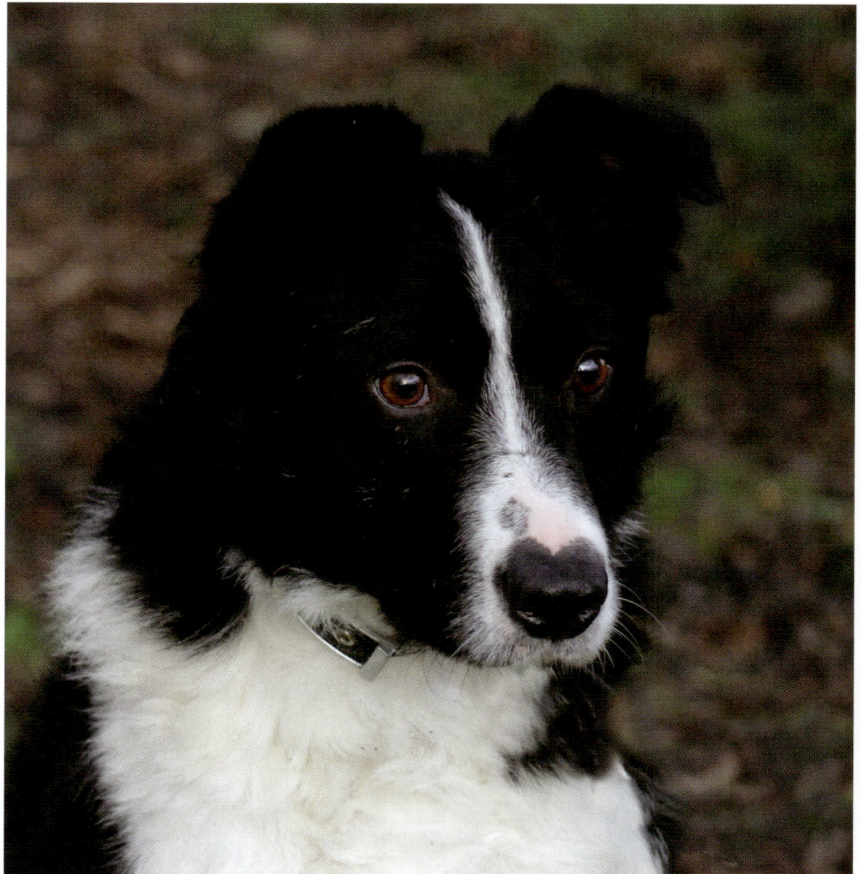

Inside this beautiful head is a bank full of memories. A dog does not recall memories at will, but certain triggers will bring memories back. A certain smell, noise or action can bring back a memory: it may be a pleasant one, or one that scares him. As you get to know your dog his memory bank will tell you a lot about his past.

Collies can become obsessive, and if they play too much or for too long they can get over-excited and then they can become possessive.

Redirecting the Chase

Chasing for a collie is against everything they have been bred to do; they are hunters and herders who love to work, and who need someone to work with. We also know they want to control movement. They can become obsessive, and they love to please, and in that order we have what we need in order to learn how to manage them. If a dog is chasing something, it will struggle to control it until the object of the chase stops. If a dog doesn't catch a ball, the ball will eventually stop, but cats, children, bikes and cars don't. To our human mind, those are five things that the dog shouldn't try to control, but dogs see things differently to us, and if they can chase after just one thing then they can chase after as many different things as they want!

The first two things that a shepherd will want to teach his dog are a stop and a recall. Without those, the first time the dog sees the sheep it will want to control them, but the sheep will run and that will leave the dog chasing after the sheep. He will also either have his dog on a long training line as back-up, or will work in a very small area with a small number of sheep. Without the space to run to, the sheep will stand close together, thus giving the young dog time to stop and think, and to go round them in order to gain full control.

Why am I talking about training for sheep work? Because Border Collies are sheepdogs, and the training

Using a ball to teach a dog not to chase. Buddy has seen the ball roll a short distance and has been made to sit and wait, but when he is walked forwards he wants to set off to get the ball.

Buddy is stopped and is not allowed to go forwards again until he calms down.

Finally he can get the ball. Eventually he will learn that the calmer he remains, the more likely he is to get the ball – but he will also learn that sometimes when he is sent off for the ball, he will be stopped and brought back to his guardian.

that teaches them to herd and not chase, to observe but not always take part, to watch but not always take control, is the same training needed in a companion home. However, there are no sheep in the home, so we need to use other methods to tap into the working mind of the collie to be able to control it. Anything that encourages or allows a collie to give chase needs to be put on hold until he has been taught how to observe.

If a dog is used to running after a ball, a good way of redirecting the chase is to use the ball not as a distraction, but by teaching a dog *not* to run after it. Dogs taught to fetch balls repeatedly can soon become obsessed with them. Here we need to remember the three stages of the collie's mind: attempt to control, become obsessive, happy to please; and we must also remember the first two necessary instructions: 'stop' and 'come back'.

You need to have your dog on a lead, and instead of throwing the ball, just roll it a few yards. At this stage, the collie who is on an eye level with the ball is anxious to run in case the ball doesn't stop, which is why it's important to roll it only a short distance. When the ball does stop, walk your dog on the lead to the ball, teaching him a 'steady' command as you go, and then let him pick it up. If you refrain from throwing the ball and make this a regular exercise, rolling the ball a bit further each time, you are teaching your dog that he can't set off to control something without your permission.

The next stage is to have your dog on a long line, and with the 'steady' command, let him go towards the ball, then 'stop' him, then tell him to 'come back' to you (choose your own words, whatever are best for you and your dog), and with the long line, make sure he comes back straightaway. Once he is back with you, praise him and have a few moments quality time with him, then let him go for the ball. Your dog will learn that he doesn't run after something moving without permission, and if he does, he has to respond immediately to the commands to 'stop' and 'come back', if they are given, when he will be able to spend some time being stroked and massaged.

Collies love to learn new things, and if this is kept simple, they will soon be masters at it. However, this does require patience and simplicity. The dog's memory bank will remember how he left his last game, and if you finish by throwing the ball and letting him chase after it, that is what he will remember.

In order for our dogs to learn, we need to put aside what we want and accept that they need time to absorb new information, and if something else is thrown into the mix, they will stop learning and start to get wound up. Once your dog has learned how to control his desire to control the movement, he can go after the ball when it is thrown, as long as every so often you do a 'refresher' course. Go where there are other dogs and children playing, and sit down with him. Remember, he's been taught not to chase without permission, so now, when he stares at something, teach him to 'leave it' and to redirect his gaze to you so you can stroke and massage him. I believe that, quite apart from helping your dog to control his instincts, the time spent together learning new things is more fun that endless ball throwing.

Living Without a Ball

I have to admit that I don't throw balls for my own dogs, but that doesn't mean we don't interact, that I don't love them, that we don't have fun, or that they are missing out on anything. They can, and some of them will, play with a ball in the garden, but sometimes they are just not interested, preferring to be with me or to go for a walk.

Most farm dogs don't understand balls, and sometimes guardians get frustrated trying to make their dogs play, but these dogs are used to amusing themselves and are quite happy just to be someone's friend.

A dog seeing a ball for the first time doesn't pick it up and take it to his guardian and demand he throws it for him. In fact, if one is thrown, he is more likely to think someone is throwing it at him and not for him. Dogs can learn to be ball obsessive when they are pups, but if they are taught the above rules from the start, they will learn to play ball calmly, and any urge to chase other movement will be controllable.

Dogs from farms won't have seen a ball, and they won't understand why people seem so fascinated in them – and from the dog's point of view, constantly throwing the ball away must seem like a strange pastime. To us, it's a ball. To a dog, it's an object with no apparent purpose. But if encouraged to interact with the ball, with this bringing them lots of praise, they will happily turn into a ball chaser – and before long they will be ball obsessive.

I have to confess, when people proudly tell me that their collie is ball obsessive, I picture the amazing, gentle suppleness and the intelligence of the breed, and then picture the much less flowing movements and the obsession of the ball chaser, and I feel sad. There is so much more to their beautiful minds, when they watch sheep, other dogs, people, when they observe. They are thinking – but there is no thought in chasing a ball. However, there are other great ball games, which are covered in Chapter 15.

The 'Leave' Command

If a dog has been abused or is very nervous, it is highly likely that he will never feel brave enough to try and control movement, but a dog with a keen eye will want to stalk. Quite often these dogs will stand staring, almost glued to the spot, and getting their attention will be difficult, especially if he is an amber-eyed dog. He probably won't run after anything moving slowly, preferring to try and control it just with his eye power; however, if he does decide to run to the object of his stare, he won't know what to do when he gets there. When entering the space of a sheep that doesn't move, he has no alternative but to nip it to make it move, and if the object of his focus looks directly at him, his amber-eyed gene will tell him he is being threatened. This dog needs a 'leave' command, which isn't hard to teach, but like all other instructions, it needs to be taught where there are no distractions.

Start with something simple – for example your dog looking at a bird in the garden, a horse or a sheep on a

Ben and the 'Leave it' Command

Ben was a soft-eyed dog who had been attacked by other dogs, and was so scared of being attacked again that he became aggressive towards any other dog. When he stared at them, it wasn't to stalk or to control, it was through fear. When Ben came into rescue, due to his aggression, it soon became obvious that he felt he had to protect himself. In his eyes, he had been attacked several times, and no person had managed to make him feel safe, and that wasn't going to change overnight. When he saw another dog he became aggressive, and no amount of persuasion could distract him. However, his weakness was biscuits, so when his handler saw another dog before Ben had time to focus on it, he was shown a biscuit. Then he was led forwards at a brisk walk with his eye on the biscuit, and while the other dog passed, he was told he was a good lad and given the biscuit while he was being stroked. This progressed to him not being shown the biscuit, but still being given one while he was being stroked after the other dog has passed by.

Eventually he could be told to 'leave it' when he saw another dog, and he would walk away while being told what a good lad he was, and no biscuit was needed. It took several weeks of patience, and of finding calm dogs to walk past him, but he changed from an angry dog shaking with fear, to a dog who could walk past other dogs.

walk, a leaf that floats to the ground, anything that grabs his attention. Remember, you can't ask a dog not to do something without giving him an alternative behaviour. The moment his attention goes to something, ask him to 'leave it' and walk away (he does need to be on a lead). As soon as his attention is diverted, get his attention on you, and as he looks at you, tell him, 'look at me'. In his eyes, he has put his attention on something that he thinks he should control, but you have walked him away from it with the 'leave it' command, and once he diverts his

As an alternative to throwing a ball, teach your dog how to 'find' a special toy. Start by dropping it in sight, then when he's really keen to find it, hide it when he's not looking, but keep him calm and let him work to find it.

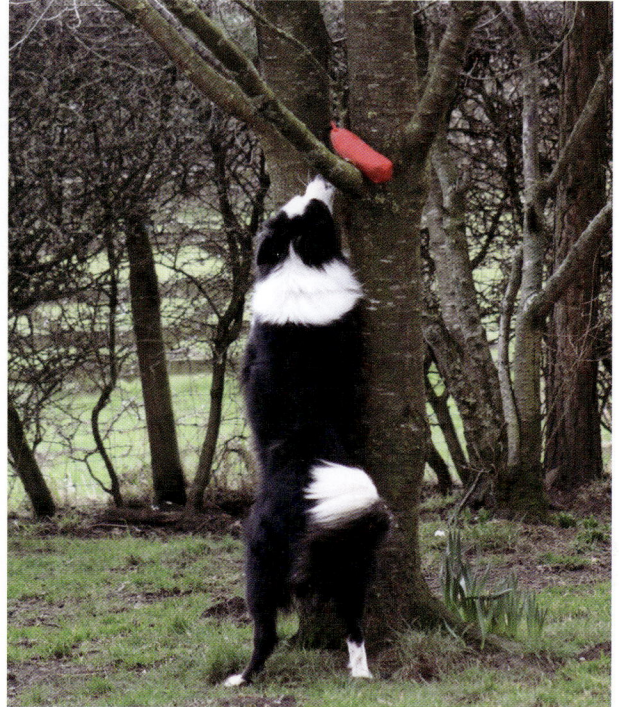

If your dog doesn't like relinquishing the toy when he's found it, put it where he can indicate where it is, then you retrieve it and give him a reward. A simple game, but your dog will be using his brain.

attention to you, he is praised and stroked. The wish to stalk is not appreciated by you, but the attention on you gives him pleasure.

Once again, this is something that needs time, patience and consistency, and he has to understand he pleases you by leaving and not by the stalking. If he is given praise the minute he takes his attention off the object of the stalk, then he will think he needs to stalk to get the praise. He will remember the last actions, so looking at you gets him praise. Eventually you will be able to roll the command into one – 'leave it and look at me' – but that is a long way down the line.

All dogs respond differently to different situations: the key thing is to find out a way to communicate with your dog. I don't train with treats. I want to be able to understand my dogs, and to give them a reason to like me for who I am, and not as a food or toy provider. But in Ben's case, it was the gentler and kinder way as he was already treat orientated, so it meant his rehabilitation could be

speeded up for his sake, as he was so scared. As Ben was learning some trust, he also learned to love the massaging he got for being a good lad, and an edible treat was no longer needed. There are no miracle cures; Ben will never be a dog that loves being with other dogs, but he doesn't need to. What he needed was to feel safe, and with the alternative behaviour learned, he could go for a walk without feeling fear.

Avoiding Stress

The dogs in sanctuary at our rescue are there because of poor health or behavioural issues. The human emotion is to feel sorry for dogs not having a home of their own or a cosy bed by a fireside, and yet those dogs in the rescue are so happy: they are well fed, kept very clean and have comfy beds, plus they have no pressure put on them. They have gardens to play in every day, covered play areas for bad weather, and they frequently get short walks or a run in a paddock. They don't have to go out in the rain, they can play with one of the various balls in the play pens, or they can just take time out to graze the herbage in the gardens or relax in the sun. Those dogs have flourished, they are in good condition, they rarely incur any vet bills, and they grow to a ripe old age. The things that sometimes we think they must have in order to be happy are not always necessary or as important as reducing the stress in their lives. My own dogs are not in kennels, they are in my home, they are my best buddies, they have the fireside and the warm home and all the things that those sanctuary dogs don't have.

Having worked with problem dogs for many years, I try to keep them as stress free as I can. I don't always have time to walk them for miles, but I do always make time to talk to them. Goodness knows what they would think if they could understand everything I said! I do know they react to my emotions, so I try not to overload them when I'm feeling down, as I know it can stress them. I might know it's going to be a short-lived feeling, but they don't know that. They can work sheep, but they aren't obsessed with working, they love going for walks, but don't have to, and they love any mind games I play with them, but they aren't obsessed with them. My dogs are very laid back and are my friends.

I'm not advocating that everyone should live on a farm, run a rescue and walk around talking to themselves! Just like this wonderful breed, every one of us is different, with different dreams and different expectations. We all live in different types of homes, and we will hope for different things from our lives and from our dogs. One thing that remains the same is the nature and sensitivity of the collie and its susceptibility to stress.

Because collies are so sensitive to stress, we need to learn what can cause it, so we need to ask ourselves why we do certain things. It's the human part of the partnership that decides which activities to instigate and whether or not to compete. Why do we throw a ball? Many people will move heaven and earth in order to get their dog to fetch the ball back each time they throw it. They will try to throw it faster each time, and will sometimes employ a thrower to make it go even further. Once the dog realizes this is what is wanted from him, he thinks it's great, he gets to really stir up his adrenalin by chasing after the ball again and again, and each time he brings it back to his guardian, he is happy and he gets praise – a double bonus for him!

At this point you are probably thinking I am being hard, that dogs do love to play ball, and that I'm being a spoilsport. We don't throw children into the sea: we teach them how to swim in shallow water first. We don't let children cook a meal: first of all we have to teach them how to cook and how to be safe. We can't let a collie try to control movement until we've taught him how and when to ignore it. We need to monitor the dog's stress levels by

However busy you are, always make time for some quality time with your dog. You don't have to be entertaining your dog all the time: special moments shared between you are important to a dog and are the foundation for a very special bond.

A dog doesn't know about any other dog's life, it only knows its own. The dogs in sanctuary don't know about firesides, but they are happy, content and stress free. The dogs that have a warm fire to lie in front of have home comforts, but often more stress. Collies think and work better when they are calm and stress free.

playing while he is calm, but if he shows signs of getting over-excited or obsessive, stop the game.

Dogs don't go shopping and choose the toys they have, and they are often quite happy with just one scruffy, smelly one. Dogs aren't interested in competing in any of the disciplines, including sheepdog trials. We are the ones that want to do it, and although Max (*see* Chapter 2) wasn't stressed, he made it quite clear he wasn't interested in doing it. Understanding the breed and getting to really know our dogs before deciding what is right for them is paramount for a great relationship, but we also need to accept that what we want isn't as important as what is best for them.

Summary

Collies are sensitive but they are also very quick to learn, and if they control movement their way, one day they will expect that that is the way to do it every other day. It would be wrong to deny them using their instincts, but they need to be managed in a way that fits into your life and family without confusion to the dog. Once your dog understands what he can and can't do, he will be ready for learning new things, but we need to remember that his memory bank can bring things to him that we don't even know exist.

CHAPTER 13

Lead Walking and Recall

I never try to teach anything without looking at it from a dog's point of view; the more we can see the world through their eyes, the easier it is to understand them. It's very easy to create a problem before there is one. Quite often people with problem collies tell me their dog pulls on a lead, but that is to be expected because that's what they do. If we think that's what they do then we won't stop them, because in our minds it is normal. But it isn't, because they only know what we allow them to do. They are used to following their mother; they are safe when they are behind her because she is in control, she leads the way, she tells them which way to go, and she finds a designated safe play area for them. In other words, she is not just their mother, she is their protector. They are safe with her, and as long as she is in front protecting them, they have nothing to fear.

This tells us what the dog expects from us, and the benefits to be gained by providing the leadership and protection they need. It also tells us one other very important thing: the one who takes the lead is the decision maker. There is a big difference between 'taking' the lead position or being 'given' it. If a dog assumes the lead from the first step of a walk, it has 'taken' it, but if the guardian takes the lead position and then gives the dog permission to walk ahead, it has been 'given' it.

From the Dog's Point of View

It's all quite simple for a dog, if they do something, they will think they can keep doing it. If we want to tell them they can no longer do it, they have to learn to forget the action they think they can do in order to learn another.

If a dog goes in front and pulls on the lead, it will assume that is the way to walk. In order to get it to walk at your side on a lead without pulling first, you have to explain to it that it must not pull, then you have to teach it how to walk correctly. It's much easier and a lot fairer on the dog to not encourage it to pull in the first place. Of course nobody sets out to encourage their dog to pull on a lead, but we have to see it from the dog's point of view, and looking at some of the methods I have witnessed, I can see why a dog would not only pull, but would think it was the right thing to do.

When the dog goes in front, the handler brings it back to the side and says 'good dog'. The dog is getting praise for the whole action, because it had to pull in order to be brought back and receive the praise. If the handler changes direction when the dog pulls, a collie will soon see this as a game. If the handler stops when the dog pulls and does nothing, the dog gets bored and either comes back to the side or carries on walking, then it sees something exciting and pulls again. However, none of these methods are actually telling the dog not to pull, as they are all implemented after the dog has pulled. Collies are very intelligent, and even if they pick up the general idea, they can still try to use it to their advantage by walking with you and receiving praise and treats. But as soon as they see another dog, they launch themselves forward, instigating an even more powerful pull than before.

It can be difficult to control a dog that is pulling, and while putting a harness and a face attachment on it might make things easier for the handler and might even ease the pulling, they are not teaching the dog not to pull, they are preventing it. Therefore they are not giving the dog the reassurance a dog seeks from a parent figure. Collies

The minute the dog gets to the end of the lead, look how he throws his weight into his shoulders: Mac is now taking control, and if another dog or person approaches, in his mind he has the right to make a decision on how to respond to them. This can't be pleasant for either dog or handler.

Good lead walking cannot be achieved until the dog is taught not to pull. If the dog is stopped before he reaches the end of the lead and consequently begins to pull, the handler is in control.

The handler remains still until the dog relaxes, and then the tension on the lead is eased. This can take a lot of time and patience, as you will be repeating the action several times and not actually going anywhere. But as long as you are consistent and don't let the dog take up the pull, it will be worth it.

are free-spirited beings: their instincts require them to be able to move freely and with suppleness, their senses of sight, smell and hearing are all linked, and if they are not looking straight ahead, they have no way of knowing what lies in front of them. Whilst pulling on a collar and lead causes pressure on the throat, so does any other form of lead connection: it can cause pressure on whatever part of the body it is attached to. A dog walking nicely on a loose lead is a joy to be with.

Lead Walking

From the previous section, we can see that if a dog commits to an action, that action is logged in its memory and is perceived to be 'normal'. We need to show dogs what we need, and not let them literally walk into something we don't want. We need to start in front, as their mother or an older group member would, and instead of using words they don't understand, use our body language. Dogs quickly pick up messages sent by body language. Don't let your dog go out of the door in front of you, but instead of using words, use your body. If you tell your dog to sit, he is responding to the command, not to stepping back and letting you go first. If you block the door or gateway with your body and don't let him pass you, he will eventually stop trying. At that point, you tell him what he is doing: 'wait'. Then either step through first, or move to one side and let him go: either way, *you* have taken control.

Two weeks into his lead walking and Mac is a more relaxed dog, and lead walking is a pleasure. Every walk is started with the dog standing behind his handler; note the lead is behind the handler's back.

Mac has learned that when the hands drop to the side he can walk at the side; he needs to be able to walk at either side.

133

The lead is still behind the handler's back, so if Mac decides to try and pull he can't pull her over.

Start your walk with your dog behind you and with your hands behind your back. Stand still and gently use your body to keep him behind you: you can do this by a fence or a wall to help make it easier for you, and you need to be very patient and wait until he is settled – then let him walk to your side on a loose lead. Never let your dog get to the end of the lead. A nice length is two metres, as this gives a dog room to move freely before nearing the pull distance. Once he gets to the pull end of the lead he will throw his shoulders into it and pull as hard as he can, at which point *he* has taken control. If you stop him before he reaches that point, his shoulders don't go into the pull position. In other words, his brain does not pick up the information that says he needs to pull harder: instead, he is being made to check his distance from you as you pause him and walk on past him.

If you have to keep repeating this action, you need to stop and keep him behind you for a few moments to think about it. You are appealing to the simplicity of the

As Mac shows signs of settling to being a good lad he is given the full lead. Note how relaxed the hander's hands are: tense hands pass a message of stress to the dog.

Still relaxed, and Mac has changed sides again. Always change sides with your dog behind you – if you let him pass him front of you he is back in control; also, changing sides from behind you slows him down and makes him think.

collie mind: 'If I am behind you, then you must be my mentor and protector. If I go in front and think about taking that position from you, then I don't get to go any further forwards. Therefore, if I want to go for a walk, I do it the way you want me to.' Believe me, this works, as you are communicating with your dog in a way he understands. But it can only work if you are patient and consistent.

When rehabilitating a dog for rehoming we have to make sure it will walk nicely on a loose lead. To be successful can mean several days, and in some cases weeks, of patience. If we are not consistent, we won't succeed. While we are doing this training they get free running exercise in the garden, or a field, or any open space on a long line. But collies are bright little beings, and when they are adopted, they will try their luck with their new guardian. If they are allowed to pull in the first week they will assume that it is acceptable behaviour with that person – a person who is now not seen as a parent figure. Interestingly, if the guardian comes back with their dog for a refresher course the dog will happily walk on a loose lead with the person who trained it.

Being consistent with the training is vital for good results. Mac is now relaxed on a long lead and enjoying the sniffs along the way, but he is working from behind or to the side rather than in front.

135

Recall

The first questions I ask people who have a problem collie, are: Does he pull on a lead? Does he have an unreliable recall? And what is he fed on? A dog that pulls on a lead will have an unreliable recall, and if there is a behavioural problem I can guarantee I will get a 'yes' to these two questions. Furthermore in 90 per cent of the cases, the dog's diet will need adjusting to help calm it down. Never underestimate the power of a ten-metre training line: letting a dog loose that doesn't have a recall, or when you are trying to teach it one, is an accident waiting to happen. For one thing, you will be calling the dog back as it runs in the opposite direction, so the dog hears the sound of the recall as he is running away from you, and not to you. Never let a collie have the option of unwanted behaviour: take away the options you don't want and leave the one that you do, and he will learn quickly.

With a child you have a shared language so you can negotiate, but for a collie, negotiation before the boundaries are established implies that you don't mean what you say. Most collies are opportunists, and if you give them

Limiting Options

If you give a child the option of several different outfits to wear, they will want them all but will probably choose the one you least want them to choose. If you give that same child a choice of just two items, they will still struggle, but will eventually decide on one. If that child is given only one item to wear they have no choice. They may argue, but the option to choose is not on the table. Eventually the child will learn how to choose wisely from a selection – but this does have to be learned. The dog without the option to pull on a lead will learn to walk on a loose lead and will eventually learn when it is acceptable to walk ahead and when it's safer to stay behind.

Try not to make an issue of the recall. Keep your dog on a long line and let him run back to front and side to side so he can enjoy running but is never more than the length of the line away, and don't let him pull. If you let your dog run in a straight line that is what he will do if he isn't on a lead.

When your dog comes back to you as happy as Bud is, even if you didn't call him, stop and give him the time he needs to feel he doesn't ever want to be far from you.

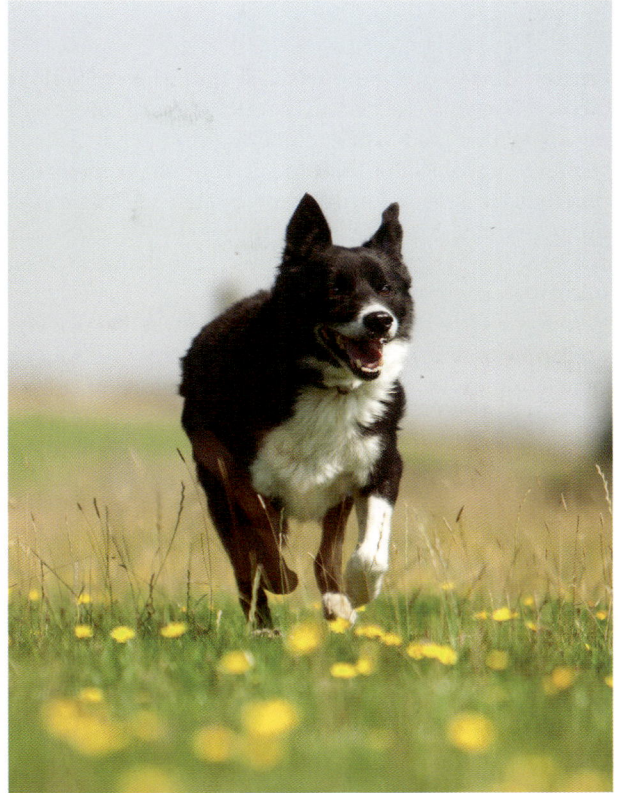

A happy recall: it is such a wonderful feeling when you know your dog wants to be with you.

a choice between what you want and what they would rather do, you don't stand a chance. Whatever you are trying to teach a dog, don't try and get it to understand the word: to a dog it's just a sound, so instead whenever it does something you want it to do, introduce the sound you want for that action. If every time a puppy runs to their guardian and hears the sound of 'that's-a-good-boy', that sound will become its recall. Notice that the words are rolled into one. Collies respond really well to lyrical sounds – for example, the words 'come' or 'here' are short, quite harsh, and easily missed, whereas something a little more musical, where each syllable can be at a different pitch, can encourage a better response – for example, 'here-to-me'.

Happy Recall

If a dog doesn't understand a recall and doesn't come back when it is called, it triggers off mixed emotions. The person calling the dog back can get anxious, frustrated and sometimes angry. The dog is happy, enjoying itself, finally comes back, and cannot understand what the fuss is about, but can feel worried, or even threatened, as he doesn't know what he has done wrong. With a puppy it is easy to start to teach the recall as he will always be running to you in the home, and each time he does, give him his recall sound. But with older dogs, and puppies who go through the adolescent phase of trying to push every boundary, employ the long line. I never have a line longer than ten metres for the recall, and I don't try to teach it

to a dog that pulls on a lead. If the lead walking is good, a dog will want to listen and learn, but if it is not good he will pull on the long line.

Let your dog wander around the garden, and call his name. If he doesn't look, give a gentle tug on the line so he turns to look at you, and then encourage him to come to you, and as he is coming, give him his recall sound. Start with short distances in a calm place, and give him time to work out what you want. You can repeat his name but not his recall: you are trying to teach him to come as soon as he hears, not after two or more attempts. Don't make an issue out of it as your dog isn't going to learn it in one lesson, or even in one week. It can take weeks and months with a young dog, and if you take the line off and let him run free and he doesn't come back, you will have set yourself back weeks of training. When he comes back, sit and talk to him, stroke him and massage him, make it so it is so good with you that he'd prefer to stay rather than run off.

137

Recall from your Dog's Point of View

First of all we have to understand that when a collie is focused, nothing else exists. Their three main senses will work together and will exclude anything that doesn't belong to the object of their focus. Your chance to break that focus is when your dog's eye catches sight of something, or when his nose begins to twitch, but once your dog's ears are tuned into something other than you, then you have lost your connection with him.

A dog isn't programmed in the same way that we are; we can hear several different noises at once and we can choose which to give priority to, but all your collie's attention will be on whatever he is focusing on. It is not selective deafness, he simply won't hear you, and if he has shut you out in order to concentrate on something he deems to be more important, when he does finally hear you, he will not know you have called him several times before. Eventually he will realize that each time he does come back you are not happy – but it is far kinder for him not to have to go through that confusion by teaching him that there isn't anything more deserving of his focus than you. You should rate higher than a ball, a toy or a treat, and no treat should be higher in value than you.

Holly and the Ten-Metre Rule

Holly came into rescue as a very scared little dog and with a lot of issues. She learned to lead walk, and she learned to love giving and receiving affection; she could free run in the garden, but was always kept on a ten-metre line in the fields. One day Holly slipped through the gate and into the field – she could have run to the far end of the field, but instead she enjoyed running around but kept to the ten-metre distance, and when called she came back straightaway.

The Unreliable Recall

I struggle to think that any dog can have a guaranteed 100 per cent recall. They are dogs, and there are times when something unexpected happens to take them by surprise, and they react. It could be a cat or a bird running across their path, or a pheasant jumping out of the undergrowth that startles them, but there are some dogs that are a constant flight risk. Sometimes they are just so

There are some dogs that for reasons of fear or years of learned behaviour cannot be trusted to be off a lead. A dog on a long line can still have freedom to run and have a great life, but if you have a shadow of doubt about your dog's recall, then for his safety keep him attached to you.

nervous that the slightest noise can make them want to run, but sometimes it can be because they have done it so many times before that it becomes a habit that they enjoy doing.

It is no slight on anyone's ability to train a dog if they have one that is a flight risk, and neither is it a sign of failure if they keep that dog on a long training line. If a dog has spent several years of its life running off, even after years of training, the memory of that action can be so deep that a memory trigger can remind it of its past and cause it to run again. Rescue dogs are the most likely to have such issues, and I can think of three such dogs: they all responded well to recall training, but there was always the risk factor with them – and they were all tri-coloured dogs with light eyes! I have a deaf dog and he is always on a long line: on the moors, on the beach, or on a day out, he is attached to me. He always observes the ten-metre rule, and once when his line broke, he stopped at nine metres and looked back at me.

I would rather have my dog on a long line and know where he is, and what he is doing, than have to experience that awful feeling when your dog doesn't come back. I want to be the one that says I'm so glad I had him attached to a long line, and not the one that says 'if only'. Of course there are dogs that have a great recall, and dogs that never go far from their guardians, but if you have one of those that could be a flight risk it is better to be safe than sorry. Collies are sheepdogs, and you might have one that looks at sheep in a field and thinks, 'No thank you, I'd rather not work'; but you are more likely to have one that thinks, 'I can do that', and if he runs off and gets into the field and the sheep run, he will chase them and the result could be disastrous. Far better to be safe than sorry.

Summary

Like everything else, lead walking and recall require time and patience, and because they are so important, you need to be consistent. Start the training at home where it's calm and there are no distractions for your dog. You can lead walk and recall from room to room, in a hall, and in the garden. Encourage your dog to follow, rather than lead you, and after each session make sure that you share some quality time with him so that he wants to learn and wants to please you.

CHAPTER 14

Understanding Problems

What is not acceptable to humans can often be perfectly acceptable to a dog, if there is no understanding of the order of parenting. For example, a dog that is allowed to think it has equality status in the home will have no problem in not wanting to accept certain visitors. Human partners will discuss and deal with the situation of a guest that one of them doesn't like; however, a dog cannot discuss, but will make its displeasure obvious. Growling or nipping will not be acceptable to the guardian or the visitor, but will be perfectly acceptable to the dog, who, during its time of living in the home, believes it has the right to make such decisions. Therefore in its eyes it has done nothing wrong in barking at, or even nipping, someone whom it didn't particularly like.

We must always ask ourselves why our dogs behave as they do, and in the case of a dog taking a dislike to visitors, he clearly thinks it is his decision to make. He believes he is entitled to make decisions, but what you have to decide is his reason for wanting to make them. Is he a nervous dog who is worried by visitors? Or is he just trying to take control? The Chill Mat (see Chapter 11) will help with either of these dogs, but for different reasons. The nervous dog needs to know that he is safe and that you are looking after him, and the assertive dog needs to know that you are the one in control. The nervous dog is just scared, but he shouldn't be. A child should feel safe in their home, and so should a dog. He may have his bed to retreat to, but if that is in view of the visitors he will feel threatened. If his bed is out of sight he will feel safer, but he isn't going to learn that his home is somewhere to feel safe.

The Dog's Point of View

Whether nervous or assertive, for the dog to think it is in control means it is sharing responsibility of the home – its pack area. Parenting is essential and is as important in the animal kingdom as it is in ours. I often ask people who have an unruly dog if they would let a child wander round my consulting room, pick things up and interrupt our conversation, and of course the answer is 'No, they wouldn't'. Yet their dog is on a lead sniffing all around the room, barking and trying to get their attention. It walked into the room first, so in its mind, it is now its job to check everything out. Having done that, it will then decide whether it wants to stay, or go, and if barking doesn't get it what it wants, it may feel angry and start growling. In our eyes this is all bad behaviour, but the dog believes it to be all right.

The nervous dog will try and hide; there is nothing familiar for him, and there are new smells that he doesn't recognize and which could mean danger in the area. These dogs are not behaving out of character – they will display the same traits at home, but it isn't as easily recognizable because it only comes to light when a normal routine is disturbed. In their eyes they are in control, and when things change in the home, they set wheels in motion on how to deal with it, and this can mean running into a corner or taking assertive action.

Always take time to look at the world through your dog's eyes, mentally and physically. The human eye sees houses, trees, and a view into the distance.

This is the dog's eye view: nothing much but grass to see, and it will probably smell interesting. If this was your view, imagine how you would feel if a person, another dog or a toddler were approaching.

A collie's tail is a vital part of his body language that we need to 'listen' to. Right leg forward, tail at 'half mast' and to the left – balance.

Head up, ears up and tail up, this dog is not nervous: the eyes have seen, the ears are listening and the tail, which is stiff and with no bend in it, says that if he doesn't like it he will take action.

Understanding your Collie

Because collies are so diverse, it is impossible to give a simple solution to any problem. Just like us, they are all in need of being understood for their individuality. Teaching children will require the same parenting principles for each child, but parents will also need to understand each child as an individual. The principle of understanding and teaching collies is the same for each one: you need to be the leader or the parent figure, but you will also need to know which ones are going to be stubborn, which are overly sensitive, and which are going to try and outsmart you at every turn.

The training for a medium-coated, black-and-white, hazel-eyed collie will be the same as for a short-coated, tri-coloured, amber-eyed collie, but the application of that training will need to be different. One is going to try and please you, and the other is going to try and make you prove you are worth pleasing. One will try hard to learn, and the other will either turn into a quivering jelly, or will argue with you from start to finish. Do you know which is which?

The following sections are examples of some problems,

143

A dog running and having fun, but the tail says his mind isn't concentrating: he isn't thinking, but it is a relaxed tail so he's having fun.

A dog running with the tail down in the thinking position: the body is relaxed and the dog is concentrating on something.

but the answers to solving them will depend on the type of collie. Look at the problems and see if you can work out how each different collie would respond, and think how you would need to adjust for a collie with a different nature to the one in the text. The answers to most problems lie within the chapters of this book.

My Collie Refuses to Walk Forwards

There will be more problems than just refusing to walk forwards, and to find them there are questions that need to be answered. What colour is he? What is he fed on? Does he pull on a lead normally? How long have you had him? How are you dealing with it? And how long has this been going on? The answers to these questions will provide an outline of the dog, and why it is not happy going for a walk. We know they need parenting, so things in the home may need changing, such as providing a safe place, such as a Chill Mat. And don't allow visitors to invade the dog's space.

The guardian is usually coaxing the dog with a voice completely different from their normal tone and offering titbits, and when that doesn't work, the dog goes back 'home' to his safe place. From the dog's point of view, he is scared and the person who is supposed to protect him seems as nervous as he is. If he pulls back he is given a reward and goes back home – job finished! He didn't enjoy it, but it was only a few yards, he got a treat, and he's back in his bed now, but is still terrified. His memory of that incident is of being scared and getting a treat for being scared.

This is a regular problem that we are faced with solving – but have you thought about which collie is most likely to behave this way? They are usually always short coated and with pricked-up ears. All the inside changes need to be addressed, but the dog also needs to have a happier memory of going out for a walk.

The guardian needs to be watching the dog closely, and the moment before the dog is about to stop or pull back, he needs to be brought forwards for at least two or three steps – but the voice accompanying this action needs to be firm as well as gentle, with a 'Come on, one more step, well done!' Then stop and give lots of attention and praise, and walk back 'home' – but don't let the dog get to the pull end of the lead: if he does, stop him, walk to his side, give more praise, and set off again. The important part of this is preventing the dog from going into panic mode. Get him to take the extra step before he stops, stop him on the walk back before he pulls, and finally, as he goes back into the garden, give him another fuss and a treat.

This method works, but with the knowledge you now have of the breed, which do you think would be the most difficult one to deal with? Some dogs will get over this problem completely in time, while others will learn to walk out with confidence but will always be wary of new things on a walk.

My Dog Hates Going Out of the Door

This case history describes a problem experienced by the collie Jess. It seemed complicated, as she hated going out of the door to leave the house, but once out of the garden she loved going for a walk; but on return she would then refuse to go back through the garden gate to get to the house. I asked for a video, and saw a black-and-white, long-coated collie standing in the doorway, and obviously not happy about going out. Is your mind already working out how much of this is, or is not, nervous sensitivity? Once out of the door, Jess pulled all the way down the path to the pavement, then settled down to walk nicely. But on return, she dug in her heels at the gate, then finally dragged her guardian up the path to the front door.

Sometimes it needs an outside view to see the problem, and in Jess's case it became evident that her problem wasn't with her guardian, it was with the car parked on the pathway! Jess had no reaction to cars on the road, so it was clearly that particular car.

Jess's colour genes suggests she would be willing to learn, so how would you proceed? We put the car on the roadside and encouraged Jess to enjoy the path without the car; then she needed help to get to like the car when it wasn't on the path; and finally we put them all together for the final stage. As always, there is no quick fix, and it wasn't something that could be solved in a week. It took a lot of time and forethought first to remove the car, then to make sure Jess didn't see it on the pathway until we thought she was ready for that stage. But the length of time and dedication needed was worth it when Jess trotted happily down the path past the car.

Sometimes the answer to a problem isn't always obvious until you view it from a different angle. It's always worth taking a video of yourself with your dog to get a different perspective. Do you think a tri-coloured, short-coated dog would have been as forgiving? Or might it always have remained a little reserved walking past the car? And would that dog have been fine with cars on the road? Or would it have been reactive to the movement?

My Dog is Aggressive to Other Dogs

Dogs can be aggressive to other dogs through fear or for power. In Chapter 12, Ben had become aggressive through fear, but it had turned to a feeling of power. In all cases of aggression the dog needs removing from temptation, or from its fear, until a bond of trust has been nurtured between the dog and the guardian. If this means garden exercise only while the lead walking, the standing behind, and the trust are built up, then so be it. A dog on garden exercise can be happy if the guardian is working with them and building a solid relationship, but a dog going out for walks where it is constantly either scared or is looking to scare another dog, is an unhappy dog in need of boundaries and parenting.

Which is going to take the longest to turn round? The black-and-white, hazel-eyed dog? The tri-coloured, short-coated dog? Or the tri-coloured, short-coated, amber-eyed dog? One of them will quickly learn the 'leave' command and will respond to being parented, one will argue and take longer to respond, and one will become manageable but will always be on the look-out for a problem to react to. Do you know which is which?

My Dog is Possessive over Food

Oddly enough, food aggression is something we rarely worry about in the rescue. Sometimes a dog will eat only half his meal, then will guard the rest until he wants to finish. Some are aggressive from the moment you try to put the dish down, but if a dog is guarding his food, it's because he thinks he is going to lose it. I've heard all sorts of remedies, from hand feeding them, to making them sit and wait before they can eat it – which is all very well, but not so good if you are at risk of losing your hand in the process! Some early training recommendations are to teach a dog to let you lift up the dish of food, then put it back down again. Food is precious to most dogs, and if they are willing to protect it, then it's very precious. I can relate to that: I still remind my son of the time he took the last scampi from my plate, and that must have been thirty years ago!

As far as I am concerned, my dog's food is there for him to eat, and I feel it would be mean to keep taking it away from him, and although I have never actually taught my dogs to sit and wait when I put their dishes down, they always do, because they are well mannered. With food-aggressive rescue dogs, we don't feed them in their pens, they are fed in a quiet play area with no other dogs around. When the food is finished, they go back to their pens. This way they can eat in peace, and they are never aggressive in their pens because we don't give them food in them.

In the home they need to be in a room on their own, and make sure the food is on the floor waiting. Don't try putting it down in front of them. With a dog that only eats half his ration, then only give him half. Don't try and give the other half later in the day, as you need to minimize risk, not create it. The dog will soon eat up all the smaller offering, then you can increase the amount you give him gradually. The habit of keeping some back for later will be broken. Only when a dog realizes that he is not going to lose his food, and that he can trust his guardian, will he become more trustworthy. You might expect that the short-coated tri-colours will be the most difficult to deal with, but they are usually far too much in love with food to leave any, and are quick enough to learn the new rules in a very short time.

I cannot stress enough not to argue with a dog that is aggressive, especially over food. There will be a reason for the behaviour, and until you have worked out what the reason is and how to manage it, try to avoid any confrontation.

My Amber-Eyed Collie Doesn't Like Children

The amber-eyed dog will stand and stare at a sheep, 'holding' it with its gaze. It will be so focused that very little will distract it, and then only for a second. This dog has a large area of personal space and doesn't like strangers approaching it inside that space. It will stare at people, almost encouraging them to make eye contact, and if they do, he won't like it.

Now put yourself in this dog's position: literally, at his height he is on the same eye level as a small child, and children tend to stare; they also have no concept of personal space, especially when it comes to a strong-eyed collie. To the collie, the advancing child staring at him, and on the same eye level, is a threat, and unless someone distracts him or moves the child, he will feel he has to make a decision. Often he will duck his head to one side and move away, but what may be one isolated incident resolved, the 'collie memory' will have it logged, and children will always be a reminder of something he does not want to be near.

Like any problem it is manageable, mainly by discouraging any contact with a child, teaching the dog the 'leave' command to ignore the child, and introducing the Chill Mat as a safety zone. The dog can eventually learn to accept a child in the family, but will probably always be wary of children who are not part of the family.

This dog is making it clear that he is not happy with a person approaching him.

As the approaching person gets nearer, it becomes too much for him: he is on a lead so he can't run away, but if he were aggressive he would be trying to bite. Note the handler's body is relaxed and not offering any confidence or protection to the dog.

Notice how the handler has taken action with his hands behind his back and using confident, protective body language.

The approaching person is much nearer now, and as the dog tries to move forwards the handler's leg shifts slightly to the left to offer more protection. The approaching person can be asked to not come any nearer.

What Should I Feed my Collie?

Whatever you decide to feed your collie it should be your choice. However, that choice should be guided by what is best for your dog. It cannot be based on what someone else feeds their dog, or the most expensive food, or the one that looks the most appealing to the human eye. A good friend might tell you how well their long-coated, black-and-white or tri-coloured collie is on a certain brand of food, but if you have a short-coated collie you might find it becomes agitated or over-excited on that same food. The dogs we see on consultations, whatever breed they are, nearly always benefit from having their diet reduced in energy. There is a saying: 'If it ain't broke, don't fix it': meaning in this context, if you don't have a problem with your dog, and it is happy and healthy, then what you are feeding is working for your dog. But if there is a problem, then consider carefully how much energy you are giving in each meal.

Collies are a very old and well established breed, and for many years they have lived and worked happily on a simple diet. They have naturally high levels of energy and stamina, the first providing impetus needed for action, and the second to keep that action going for a long time. A dog working sheep can be running for miles, and at the same time it will be working out which sheep is going to pose a problem, and how to manage that problem. When the sheep are gathered in and the collie appears to be sitting quietly in a corner, it will still be working: it will be forever watchful, and when a sheep tries to escape it will be there almost before the sheep moves.

You can walk your dog all day, and you can throw a ball until it is weary, but it will not be using the amount of energy it would use when working sheep. You may get it physically tired, but its brain will still be fresh. Have you ever wondered why, after a tiring walk, your collie will have a short nap and then be ready to go again? Now you have the answer, and you can understand why feeding a lot of energy to a dog that already has plenty, can start to cause problems.

Can my Collie Go Upstairs to Bed?

It might seem like a simple question to some, but to others it's an important one. Some guardians get upset because they have been told that a dog on a higher level than them can dominate them; that dogs on the furni-ture are taking over, and they definitely should not be in the bedroom or on the bed. I agree with all of the above, but if you have a well mannered dog with no issues, then you and your collie should live your life as you want, and not how other people live theirs – but what is important is that privileges need to be earned. By letting a young dog get on the furniture, run up and down the stairs, and sleep in your bedroom, you can actually be creating problems. My old dogs will curl up on the settee with me and will go upstairs for the night. My young dog stays downstairs, however, and she will often be out learning new things when the oldies are having a midday doze. It's about parenting, and although we may all do things differently, the end result needs to be the same: polite and well-mannered dogs.

I am not suggesting you should let your dog do all those things, but I do think that if it is what you want, then work towards it, don't just allow it to happen. A dog must be given permission to do these things, and not feel that it has the right to do them, and it needs to be mature and calm enough to be allowed such privileges.

About Breeding

A question I am often asked is, 'Should I breed from my dog?' As far as I am concerned there should only be one reason for breeding, and that is to keep a good breeding line going. I can understand someone wanting to have a puppy from their companion dog, but if the dog isn't registered there will be no idea of its ancestry in order to breed compatibly, and an understanding of the dog's genetics is needed to be able to choose the best mate.

I used to breed puppies many years ago, but only to keep my own line going. There would be one litter every three or four years. No bitch of mine ever had more than one litter, and some didn't have any. Also, no male dog was ever used for outside stud. If you have a companion dog, I would say enjoy it for the whole of its life, but don't put it through having a litter of pups if you don't need to. If you do, you are going to lose nearly a year of normal life with your dog. The last couple of months of pregnancy, your dog will need to be on low exercise. The first three months after birth she will be nursing her pups, and after weaning it will take several more weeks for her to get back into shape.

If you have a male dog I would definitely say don't use him for stud for the sake of having a pup, as once he has done what is needed to become a dad, you might find your companion dog's attitude to other dogs changes dramatically.

Can I Teach my Dog to Work Sheep?

Would you take a child into a sweet shop, let them see what is on offer, and then tell them they can't do it again? It takes a long time to fully train a dog to work sheep, and you need regular access to sheep. If you take your dog to sheep but he is not going to have regular training, the next time he sees some he's going to want to work them, but he won't know how and will end up chasing them. My answer is always the same: don't stir up the instinct of a young dog to work when he isn't going to be trained to work sheep.

Summary

It is in a collie's nature to test the boundaries, especially when they are young. They are intelligent and mischievous, which is a combination guaranteed to keep us on our toes. But once you understand the different characters, and you start to see the world as a collie would see it, you will find problem solving much easier. If things aren't going right and your dog has developed an issue, there will be a reason for it. Before trying to solve the problem, sit back and take some time out to work out the why and the when. Once you have at least one of those answered, you are halfway towards solving the problem.

CHAPTER 15

The Amazing Border Collie

To know this breed is to love it, and the fun you can have with a collie just gets better the more you understand him. You may have felt while reading this book that I am against balls and toys. I'm not against them, but I have seen far too many collies put at risk by being given too much, too soon, causing them to become over-excited and obsessive. Racing after a ball can encourage chasing and tugging at their lead, and toys can incite biting – although by now you should have a good idea which type of collie is likely to be most reactive. Sometimes we ask our dogs to do things that fulfil our desires, but it isn't always in their best interest even though it comes from a place of love and caring. If these things are not benefiting your dog, you need to find a different approach.

Fun and Games

Hide and Seek

There are many ways you can have fun without winding up your dog, and games that include you, more than throwing a ball, will achieve this. Teach him how to 'search' for a special 'search toy' – most of our rescue dogs love this game, but we keep it very calm. We will walk round the garden and drop the toy under a bush or in thick grass, and then show the dog empty hands. We don't encourage with an excited voice, but we do have a word for when they are near it, and one for when they are going in the wrong direction.

If a dog isn't interested in this game, we try something else. Hide and seek in a securely fenced area is good. Once the dog learns to 'find' someone, we exchange the person for an item of their clothing. And after that we give them a scent of something we have hidden, and off they go looking for it. Again, not all the dogs like it, but those that do have great fun, and are using their brains to work out where to go. We have huge unbreakable balls that they have fun trying to pick up, and when they can't, they find a way to roll them round the garden entertaining themselves.

Push Ball

This game takes patience to teach, but it is good fun and great for wet weather as it is a good indoor game. My usual version of this is lying on my stomach facing my dog and pushing the ball towards him with a 'no teeth' command – not 'leave', as I don't want my dog to leave it. The dog has to figure out how to return the ball to me without picking it up. Mossie used to push it back with her nose, but Tess will push it with a paw. Because Mossie used her nose, I tried to get Tess to do the same, but she got frustrated. I soon learned my mistake, and instead of telling her what to do, I let her work out her own method. You see, we are all learning all the time, and the more we learn, the better the relationship. This game does involve being in close proximity of your dog's face, and not all dogs will respond to that, but it can be done with your feet – you can sit in a chair and push the ball to your dog's feet.

Be Creative

There are literally hundreds of dog 'educational toys' to be found in pet shops, and you can spend a fortune, but your dog may not like any of them. Try being creative and invent your own games, such as teaching your dog to

Ted is used to the 'search toy' and is now learning how to find a person – he has tracked him round the garden and the 'scent' has taken him to the fence.

Ted is convinced he is on the right track and stands up to peep over the fence, but as yet he is going by scent and is looking too far ahead.

'Are, there you are!' Ted had finally located his missing person.

The push-ball game is great for playing indoors on rainy days, but don't worry if your dog doesn't understand this game or doesn't seem to like it. Try and invent a different game that keeps him occupied and thinking.

identify different items. I would suggest you start outside until your dog learns only to identify them when asked – if not, you may end up with him bringing a lot of things to you in your home with a huge grin on his face. Be careful not to overload him with items. Start with just one, and don't progress to another until that one is firm in his memory.

The Digging Game

This game is my own invention, and every one of my dogs has loved it, but it's one for a walk, and not one for in your garden. I will bend down, lift up a stone, and look intently under it. Immediately my dog will want to know why, and what is going on? Once they get used to looking under the stones with me, we progress to my pretending to dig with my hands, and before long they are digging with me. The rules of the game are that I choose and turn over the stone, and I choose the spot to dig, and it's only for a short time – this is a great one for the beach.

I love this game. I choose a stone and pretend there is something under it – collies love to be included, so they are soon helping to get the stone up and look under it. You do need rules, such as you choose the stone and when to do it – if not, your dog will be trying to turn over every stone he sees!

A wonderful collie tail: relaxed and down in the thinking position but with a gentle curve, telling us that the brain is in gear but whatever has got his attention is not a threat.

Learn to 'Listen' to your Dog

Your dog will talk to you a lot, and to understand him you need to know his body language.

The tail between the legs means he is not happy; the tail straight down (the dead tail) means he is thinking; the tail at half-mast and relaxed means he is relaxing; the tail in the air means he is in 'giddy mode', and not thinking. You need his tail in thinking mode to teach him new things. The tail at half-mast and tense means your dog isn't happy about something and could be getting annoyed. These are examples, but you will soon learn to 'read' your dog's messages.

Quotes from the Old Shepherds

'A collie keeps its brain under its tail, and when the tail goes up, the brain drops out.' Everyone who has a collie will identify with that.

'Never train a dog in your normal voice level: it can hear you at a distance, so train to a whisper and he will learn to listen to you.'

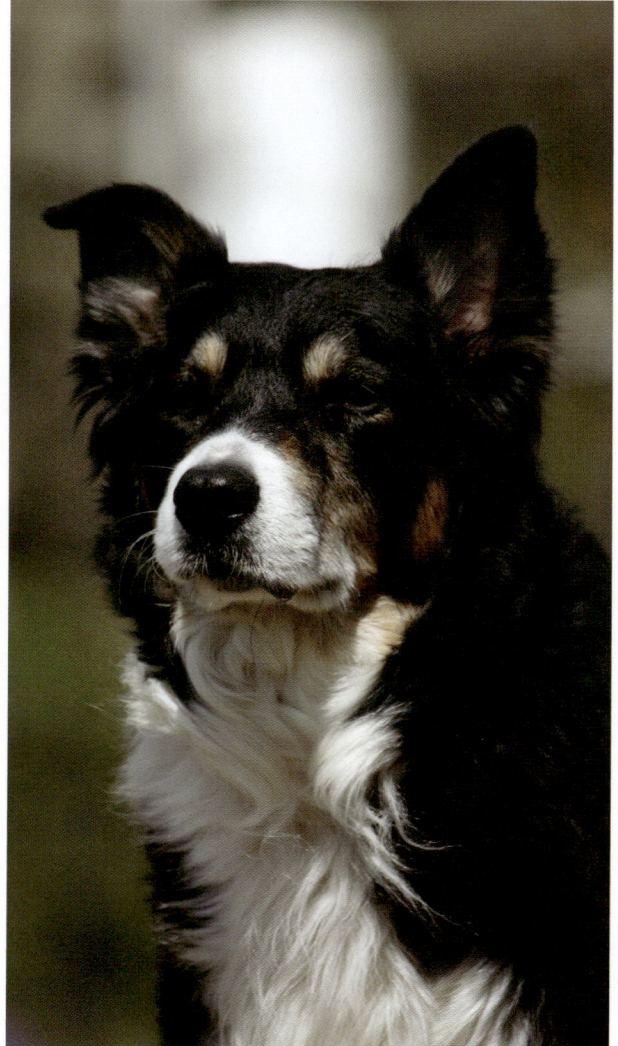

There is no age that is less perfect than another; a young dog is always ready to learn and have fun, and the wisdom of a wise old collie is something to be revered.

Living with your Collie

Collies are faithful and loving, they give that love unconditionally, and they have a wonderfully happy and simplistic attitude to life. They don't need to have expensive beds or food, and they don't need lots of toys or gadgets – they will take them if offered, but they don't need them. They need companionship, they need someone to parent them, and someone to spend their days with. They are at their happiest when they are sharing a moment with someone they love. But isn't that when we are happy? Don't just live with them, love them for what they are, no matter what character they are, whether they like people in their space or they don't – even if they have tried to test you to the limit, keep that love strong and keep parenting. The harder we have to work to get something, the more we usually appreciate it. Remember, they are not born with problems, and at some point we are going to make a mistake with our dogs – it's inevitable because we are only human, and when we do, we need to be able to recognize it, to understand our dog, apologize for the mistake, and then put it right.

The Amazing Border Collie

Your collie may not have sheep or cattle to work, but that doesn't mean he doesn't have a job to do. He has the best job of all, and one you don't have to find for him. His job is being part of your life. His work is thinking about what pleases you. He has no ego, he just wants to be able to understand what you want so he can accomplish any tasks you give him. If you have no tasks for him, his work is to sit patiently with you and to watch you, either close by or from a distance: as long as he can see or sense you, he will be happy. He doesn't need lots of gifts, he doesn't need miles of walking, he doesn't even need to be entertained. If you can be his best friend, his mentor and protector, and if needed you can let go of all you want him to do and be happy with simply having this amazing dog in your life, you will have the best friend that anyone could wish for – and when that happens, your life will be forever changed by this amazing breed.

Further Information

Useful Websites

Mainline Border Collie Centre
www.bordercollies.co.uk

Freedom of Spirit Trust for Border Collie Rescue
www.fostbc.co.uk

International Sheep Dog Society
www.isds.org.uk

Books

McCulloch, John Herries, *Sheepdogs and their Masters* (Toft East Publishing)
A history of the Border Collie

Sykes, Barbara, *Training Border Collies* (The Crowood Press)

Sykes, Barbara, *Understanding Border Collies* (The Crowood Press)

Index

Related Titles from Crowood

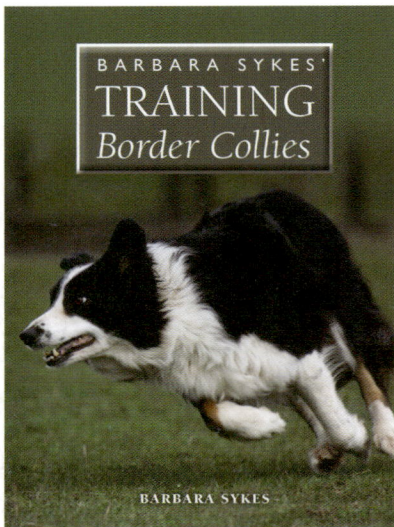

Training Border Collies
978 1 84797 889 9

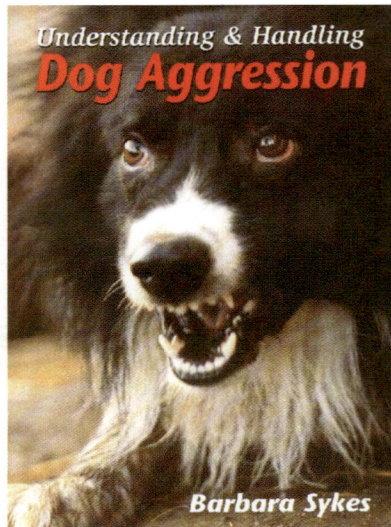

Understanding and Handling
Dog Aggression
978 1 86126 462 6

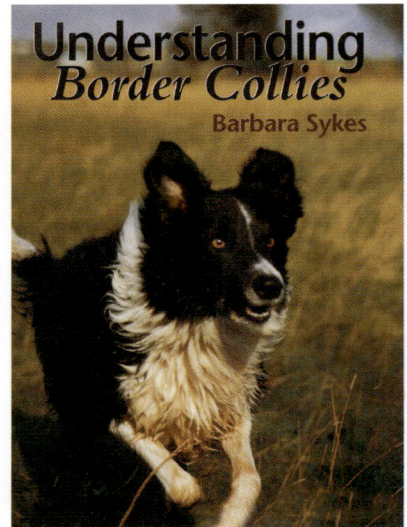

Understanding Border Collies
978 1 86126 280 6